TWENTIETH-C

DIE PHYSIKER

DIE PHYSIKER

Eine Komödie in Zwei Akten

VON

FRIEDRICH DÜRRENMATT

Edited by Arthur Taylor, M.A., M.Ed.
Deputy Headmaster, Peterlee Grammar Technical School

Nelson

Thomas Nelson and Sons Ltd
Nelson House   Mayfield Road
Walton-on-Thames   Surrey
KT12 5PL   UK

51 York Place
Edinburgh
EH1 3JD   UK

Thomas Nelson (Hong Kong) Ltd
Toppan Building 10/F
22A Westlands Road
Quarry Bay   Hong Kong

Thomas Nelson Australia
102 Dodds Street
South Melbourne   Victoria 3205
Australia

Nelson Canada
1120 Birchmount Road
Scarborough   Ontario
M1K 5G4   Canada

© Peter Schifferli, Verlags A.G. 'Die Arche', Zürich, 1962,
and A. Taylor 1966 for the editorial matter

First published by Macmillan Education Ltd 1966
ISBN 0-333-00543-0

This edition published by Thomas Nelson and Sons Ltd 1992
ISBN 0-17-439751-8
NPN 9 8 7 6 5 4 3 2

All rights reserved. No paragraph of this publication may be reproduced,
copied or transmitted save with written permission or in accordance with
the provisions of the Copyright, Design and Patents Act 1988, or under the
terms of any licence permitting limited copying issued by the Copyright
Licensing Agency, 90 Tottenham Court Road, London W1P 9HE.

Any person who does any unauthorised act in relation to this publication
may be liable to criminal prosecution and civil claims for damages.

Printed in Hong Kong

CONTENTS

	page
INTRODUCTION	vii
Dürrenmatt's early works	vii
Theaterprobleme	xvi
Romulus der Große	xxix
Die Ehe des Herrn Mississippi	xxxvi
Ein Engel kommt nach Babylon	xliii
Der Besuch der Alten Dame	xlviii
Die Physiker	liv
Conclusion	lxxii
Die Physiker	1
21 PUNKTE ZU DEN PHYSIKERN, by the author	89
BIBLIOGRAPHY	93
NOTES	95
VOCABULARY	109

INTRODUCTION

Dürrenmatt's early works

THE Second World War and its aftermath have had a stunting, inhibiting effect on all German intellectual and cultural life, especially in the theatre, where there has been, over the last few decades, an extreme paucity of new talent. Plays of international repute — one can instance Zuckmayer's *Des Teufels General*, numerous works of Brecht, and the Austrian Hochwälder's *Das heilige Experiment* — come from the pens of fairly mature authors. The 'Nachwuchs', particularly in Germany itself, has a spasmodic, ephemeral character.

Helping to fill this gap are the Swiss writers, Max Frisch (born 1911) and Friedrich Dürrenmatt (born 1921), who both gained some inspiration from Brecht's Epic Theatre, with its original approach and strong element of social criticism. It is significant that the Zürich 'Schauspielhaus', scene of many a Dürrenmatt première, was the only German-speaking stage to offer Brecht's plays during the war years: *Mutter Courage* (1941), *Der gute Mensch von Sezuan* (1942), and *Das Leben des Galilei* (1943), which, with its emphasis on the interrelation of science and humanity, may have inspired Dürrenmatt to dramatize the quandary of modern scientists in *Die Physiker*.[1]

Another writer much admired by Dürrenmatt was Thornton Wilder, whose *The Skin of Our Teeth* had a first performance in Zürich in 1944. These plays, followed by Frisch's *Chinesische Mauer* (1946), swept like a fresh breeze

[1] Cf. also Kipphardt's *Oppenheimer* (1964), which gives a factual account of the dilemma of the idealistic nuclear scientist.

into the stuffiness and solemnity of the traditionally-minded theatre, with its predilection for established classics, and laid the foundations for a modern, pulsating world theatre, such as, at the time, only Switzerland could foster. Frisch wrote of this period: 'Wir hatten sogar, was die Kriegsländer nicht haben: nämlich den zwiefachen Anblick': the Swiss dramatists, less involved and less burdened by conscience, had the vision and enthusiasm to penetrate beyond the immediate issues of the war.

Amidst this atmosphere of change and experiment in the late forties, young Friedrich Dürrenmatt found the inspiration to write his first plays and in a few years established himself as one of the leading German-speaking playwrights, praised by many, but also fiercely criticized. Of his personal life he has said 'Ich habe keine Biographie', and biographical details are indeed only incidental to an understanding of his works.

He was born in 1921 at Konolfingen, near Berne, the son of a Protestant parson. His grandfather, Ulrich Dürrenmatt, had been a rebellious political figure of some importance, whose satirical verses in the *Berner Volkszeitung* waged relentless war against all forms of corruption, materialism, and narrow-mindedness. Friedrich attended the village primary school and later a neighbouring secondary school, until in 1935 the family moved to Berne, where he completed his schooling at the 'Freies Gymnasium' and the 'Humboldianum'. After a term at Zürich University in 1941, he transferred to Berne, studying philosophy, literature, and natural sciences, but never graduated. Much of his time was spent in painting and sketching, an interest that has certainly enhanced his descriptive powers. During the years 1946–8, spent in

INTRODUCTION

Basle, he tried to keep himself financially solvent by means of plays, short stories, critical works, and cabaret sketches. The latter, with their mordant criticism of contemporary life, gave some hint of the incisive wit and biting satire of his later works.

The first of these to achieve a public performance was the Anabaptist drama *Es steht geschrieben*. This very lengthy work bears many traces of the youthful 'Sturm und Drang' mentality of the author. It consists of a series of tableaux, with admixtures of expressionism, surrealism, didacticism, and scurrility, depicting life in the besieged town of Münster during the Anabaptist rebellion in 1536. The varied characters in the crowd scenes stem from Shakespeare, but much of the dialogue has a Rabelaisian touch. The four hours' performance culminates in the famous 'Dachfirstszene', where the two main participants, dishevelled and frenzied, do a macabre dance on the rooftop, lit up by an enormous full moon with craters visible, before being put to death on the wheel. On the opening night the actors stolidly ignored the accompanying pandemonium from the audience and brought the play to a successful conclusion.

To achieve dramatic effect, and to illustrate his doctrine that man can only serve this world by a basically humble approach to its problems, Dürrenmatt often creates characters whose outlook on life drives them to some form of excess. The two main examples of this in *Es steht geschrieben* are Bernard Knipperdollinck, a wealthy Münster merchant, and Johann Bockelson, a poor tailor from Leiden in Holland. They bear more than a passing resemblance to Mississippi and St. Claude (*Die Ehe des Herrn Mississippi*) and to the blind duke and da Ponte (*Der*

Blinde). The first-named of each pair has a superabundance of either piety or self-righteousness and so falls an easy prey to the ruthless hedonism or unscrupulous idealism of his counterpart. In *Es steht geschrieben* the clash of these diametrically opposed outlooks results in a reversal of the material situation of each: Knipperdollinck renounces all wealth, his wife, and his children, for 'es steht geschrieben' that a rich man cannot enter the Kingdom of Heaven; Bockelson, who is picked up, drunk in the gutter, by road-sweepers, becomes king of the Anabaptists and obtains all the wealthy man's possessions. The tailor's hunger is not spiritual, but seeks after power, wealth, and sensual pleasures.

The third important figure is the Lutheran bishop, whose army finally overruns the town. He is a man of moderation and maturity, the voice of sanity in this world of excesses, and so comes near to the viewpoint of Dürrenmatt himself, who is described by one of the characters, in an address to the audience, as 'ein entwurzelter Protestant, behaftet mit der Beule des Zweifels, mißtrauisch gegen den Glauben, den er bewundert, weil er ihn verloren [hat]'. The bishop's belief in the virtue of humility is a frequently recurring theme in literature; its correlative — that overweening pride brings on its just punishment — is implicit in *Oedipus* and other Greek tragedies. These sentiments anticipate a person of great stature in Dürrenmatt, the Emperor Romulus, and are also found in the speeches of Akki (*Ein Engel kommt nach Babylon*) and in the postscript to *Die Physiker*.

The essentially sane outlook of the bishop stands in sharp contrast to the lack of moderation in the play as a whole, which is a grotesque mixture of very different elements. Parody abounds, farce is a concomitant of tragedy; bathos is achieved by a switch from the sublime and the lyrical to the ridiculous and scurrilous. A solemn or even tragic atmosphere is built up, often at some length, only to be destroyed by the sudden introduction of the banal and commonplace, as, for example, when the serious discussion between the bishop and Knipperdollinck is interrupted by the raucous exhortations of the 'Gemüsefrau':

'Äpfel! Äpfel! Direkt aus dem Paradies! Direkt vom Baum der Erkenntnis! Sie rutschen in den Magen und scheuern die Därme! Ganz billig!'

This device, common in Hoffman and Heine, is well exploited by Dürrenmatt and is the basis of much of his comedy.

The most exaggerated form of this debunking is the so-called 'alienation' effect, the 'Verfremdungseffekt', which owes much to expressionism and perhaps even more to Brecht.[1] It is achieved by a deliberate ignoring of all the usual theatrical conventions, so that the illusion created by the normal kind of play is considerably weakened. In *Es steht geschrieben* actors address the audience and give a preview of events, or they discuss the author's religious beliefs and his motives in writing the play. The décor has a distinctly surrealist touch, as, for instance, the enormous moon and deep-blue sky of the 'Dachfirstszene'. Another perhaps more subtle method of weakening the illusion is the repetition, with meaningful modifications, of important dialogues, which thus acquire an air of unreality and make the speakers appear as puppets.

[1] For Brecht's Epic Theatre and the 'Verfremdungseffekt' cf. his notes to *Aufstieg und Fall der Stadt Mahagonny* and *Kleines Organon*.

The original purpose of alienation was to prevent the spectator from identifying himself too closely with the characters on the stage; his mind, not emotionally involved, would be alert and critical so that the issues at stake could be viewed objectively. Whilst Brecht was loath to admit that his avowed object was to get across to the spectator a political or moral message, it is fair to assume that alienation was for him, to some extent at least, the handmaiden of didacticism. There are numerous examples of this in Brecht's Epic Theatre, but it is open to debate whether or not he would have achieved his object better without alienation.

Another effect of alienation is to give a play certain epic qualities which would be impossible in straightforward drama, or, as in Thornton Wilder's *Our Town*, with its largely imaginary setting, to concentrate the spectator's attention on the speech and actions of the players. In Dürrenmatt, alienation, as defined above, serves a variety of purposes: to produce the grotesque and the farcical; by a striking, eccentric décor, to achieve the maximum theatrical effect; by addresses to the audience and rapid scene-changes — often by the raising and lowering of back-cloths — to give an epic sweep and breath-taking pace to the action; to make any desired commentary on the play or characters. In spite of the debt to Brecht and Wilder, Dürrenmatt showed great originality in the use of alienation.

Because of its exaggerations, excesses, and long duration, *Es steht geschrieben* had but a moderate success. For Dürrenmatt it was, however, a breakthrough which taught him much about audience reaction and the judicious use of the stage. He realized that he had been treating the spectators as if they were children, and in his next play, completed in 1947 — the year of his marriage to the actress Lotte Geißler and of Wolfgang Borchert's death in Basle — he strikes a more restrained note, though the new work has much in common with its predecessor. Both are basically Christian in sentiment and in their essentials take a line somewhere between Brecht and the medieval morality plays.

Der Blinde is the story of a blind duke who imagines he has all his estates intact, in a land of peace and plenty, whereas all around him are the ruins, misery, and vice of the Thirty Years War. He hands over the management of his affairs to Negro da Ponte, an unscrupulous, more than life-size soldier of fortune, whose role is similar to Bockelson's. Though serving under Wallenstein, he tells the duke he is in the Swedish army, thus gaining the latter's confidence and respect. In a vain effort to shake the beliefs of the blind man, da Ponte exploits him unmercifully, seduces his daughter, driving her to suicide, and has his son executed. To deceive the duke, a gruesome play is enacted by the rabble at the command of da Ponte, who vainly tries to prove that nobility, idealism, and faith must in the end submit to brutishness and ruthless materialism, the only real power on this earth. After having suffered the indignity of prostrating himself before da Ponte, with a jeering crowd around him, the duke is presented with the body of his daughter, da Ponte's mistress, after her suicide. In the face of all this, the blind nobleman's faith remains unshaken and, in the much-quoted last scene, he gains moral ascendancy over his adversary, who has to admit defeat, just as the Devil had done:

DA PONTE: Ich weiche von euch tappend wie ein Blinder.
  Ihr habt mir nicht widerstanden und habt mich
    überwunden.
  Ich bin an dem zugrundegegangen, der sich nicht
    wehrte,
  denn wer mir widersteht ist mir verfallen,
  und wer sich wehrt, ist verloren.
  Ich verlasse euch nun, wie Satan Hiob verließ,
  ein schwarzer Schatten.
DER HERZOG: So geht denn von mir in Namen Gottes.

The wording in the first part of this scene is cleverly balanced off, with appropriate alterations, against the dialogue at the first meeting of the two men. This use of repetition, already referred to, helps here to introduce and round off the play: though the illusion of naturalness is lost when the duke repeats some of his earlier questions, his words seem to acquire a prophetic, other-worldly quality, quite in keeping with the part he has played and bringing into sharp focus the religious issues involved. The basic struggle in the play is between unswerving idealism and the crass materialism of da Ponte and his followers, the kind of clash inherent in Schiller's tragedies. According to Schiller's tragic theory (*Über den Grund des Vergnügens an tragischen Gegenständen*), the enormity of the duke's sacrifice and suffering must produce the maximum tragic effect. But unlike the classical Schiller, whose heroes, ignoring the world around them, found moral freedom in the realm of the transcendental, Dürrenmatt includes in his play a searing commentary on the brutality and degradation of war. In his *Friedrich Schiller: Eine Rede* he refers to the latter's aloofness in maturer years to contemporary problems, a reflection of the 'Kleinstaatlichkeit des damaligen Reiches'. If the modern writer shows a similar lack of interest, the reasons are different: the decline of patriotism, the arrival of the machine age, and the switch of power to big business, so that the individual has a feeling of impotence:

'Für den Einzelnen bleibt die Ohnmacht, das Gefühl, übergangen zu werden, nicht mehr einschreiten, mitbestimmen zu können, untertauchen zu müssen, um nicht zu untergehen, aber auch die Ahnung einer großen Befreiung, von neuen Möglichkeiten, davon, daß nun die Zeit gekommen sei, entschlossen und tapfer, das Seine zu tun.'[1]

This insistence that the artist cannot stand aside from the grave problems of our time — he refers to them in *Theaterprobleme* as 'die Wurstelei unseres Jahrhunderts' — is reflected in *Der Blinde* and indeed is fundamental in all Dürrenmatt's plays.

Der Blinde reveals, through the frequent play upon words and the sharp thrust and parry of the dialogue, that Dürrenmatt was familiar with the baroque drama and its modern exponent, Claudel, with the significant difference that the doubting Protestant had not the sheet-anchor of the Catholic religion to fall back upon. In spite of all this, especially the medieval picture of the uselessness and sinfulness of earthly striving, the implications of the play remain strikingly modern, particularly the wholesale

---

[1] *Friedrich Schiller: Eine Rede*, p. 38. 'For the individual there remains the feeling of powerlessness, of being passed over, not being able to intervene or help in any decision, of having to submerge oneself in order not to perish, but also the premonition of a great liberation, of new possibilities, the feeling that now the time has come, boldly and resolutely to make one's contribution.'

condemnation of war and the inhumanity and beastliness of those who conduct it.

Theaterprobleme

The theatre is, for Dürrenmatt, a field in which to experiment: a play was never really finished, but developed in the light of practical experience on the stage, so that the proven weaknesses of one play helped towards the perfection of the next. The extravagances of *Es steht geschrieben* led to the streamlining, conciseness, and controlled theatrical effects of *Der Blinde*. Even so, the success achieved was moderate, indicating a need for experiments in another direction. Dürrenmatt decided to turn to comedy because he saw here tremendous scope for bringing his ideas before an ever-widening audience, most of whom were ignorant of the critical problems of our time, when mankind hovers on the brink of disaster, and human values are being eroded by the surge forward of materialism and mechanization. His grounds for this volte-face are elaborated in a slender volume, *Theaterprobleme* (1954), which is also a treasure-house of witty, original, and very pertinent remarks concerning the position of the theatre and the playwright in this modern age. A careful consideration of this essay is indispensable for a correct understanding and appreciation of Dürrenmatt's plays, even though he refutes the suggestion that they are vehicles for the propagation of specific ideas.

The treatise opens with a condemnation of those critics whose forte is the categorization of art and the formulation of rules to apply to or govern art, in this case the dramatic art. The Teutonic love of pigeon-holing is well known, but the literary critic who uses such methods — and there are many in Germany — is something of an anathema to Dürrenmatt. Such critics try to deduce their laws from the intensely personal creation of the artist, who precedes and certainly does not need these laws, generalizations, or categories, even if they happen to be right. Criticism of art in all its forms is for Dürrenmatt a barren exercise.

The stage is an instrument on which to play, not a field for theories, philosophies, or the utterances of weighty pronouncements. The Swiss dramatist's works are first and foremost about people; because they are people, they may have something to say on important matters, but for the writer the essential thing is that they become living persons, in whose life he shares — he must be 'beteiligt'. For the critic the play is an 'object': he sees only the end-product of the playwright's efforts and sufferings.

As art and the artist must take precedence over any criticism, it follows logically that the unities of time, place, and action, formulated by Aristotle and aiming at maximum precision, conciseness, and simplicity, had their origin in the Greek drama, which was itself firmly bedded in the cultural and religious background of the time:

'Nicht die Einheit des Aristoteles macht die griechische Tragödie möglich, sondern die griechische Tragödie die Einheit des Aristoteles.'[1]

However abstract an aesthetic rule may appear to be, it must have its origin in works of art.

If an action has to take place on the same spot, within a matter of hours, it follows from this restriction that it must have a 'Vorgeschichte' to achieve the most concentration of action in the least time. Such a recapitulation assumes

[1] *Theaterprobleme*, p. 11.

greater importance if the audience is unfamiliar with the subject-matter of the play. In this respect the Greeks were lucky:

'... die Zuschauer kannten die Mythen von denen das Theater handelte, und weil diese Mythen allgemein waren, etwas Vorhandenes, etwas Religiöses, wurden auch die nie wieder erreichten Kühnheiten der griechischen Tragiker möglich, ihre Abkürzungen, ihre Gradlinigkeit, ihre Stichomythien und ihre Chöre und somit auch die Einheit des Aristoteles.'[1]

As soon as the theatre lost its mythical or religious significance, the unities were altered or discarded; the audience began to pay more attention to subject-matter than to treatment; the simplicity of the Greek dramas, which brought with it depth and intensity, gave way to plots which were elaborate and involved, but not as searching.

Dürrenmatt's deduction from these arguments, some of which go back to Herder and Lessing, is that each age has its chances, its own particular background and problems:

'Die Kühnheiten des einen sind nicht die Kühnheiten des andern. Jede Kunst nützt nur die Gelegenheiten ihrer Zeit aus, und eine chancenlose Zeit wird es nicht so leicht geben!'[2]

[1] *Theaterprobleme*, p. 13. '... the spectators knew the myths the theatre dealt with and because these myths were generally known — something already in existence, something religious — the unique boldness of the Greek tragedians became possible, their abbreviations, their directness, their stichomythia and their choruses and so the unity of Aristotle.'

[2] Ibid., p. 13. 'The boldness of the one is not the boldness of the other. Each art makes the most of the opportunities of its period, and it is unlikely that there will be a period without opportunities.'

This does not imply that Aristotle's unities are completely outmoded. What was once a rule may now be an exception, as for instance in the one-act play, where the situation rather than the 'Vorgeschichte' dominates and the unity is still preserved. (These remarks could apply to *Die Physiker*, where the unities are closely observed and the situation is of more consequence than happenings prior to the opening of the play.)

A dramatic theory is, then, according to Dürrenmatt, tied to a definite cultural, historical, or religious background and hence only relatively valid. There is the Greek theatre and, to quote a modern example, Brecht's Epic Theatre, which had to include the Communist philosophy, but luckily the poet Brecht takes over from the Communist Brecht, greatly enhancing the quality of his plays. This touches on the delicate problem of the place of didacticism in art, if indeed it has a place, and corroborates Dürrenmatt's first assertion: a play must be based in some measure on the background of the times, but the dedicated personal approach of the artist is of overriding importance. His keen sense of the theatre demands directness: the writer must shun no devices and use all his cunning to make the greatest and most immediate impression on his audience:

'Ein Theaterstück wird durch das Theater, indem man es spielt, etwas Sichtbares, Hörbares, Griefbares, damit aber auch Unmittelbares.'[1]

This leads him to a condemnation of the traditional theatre, where there was no link between audience and stage, and a bewailment of the fact that the modern

[1] Ibid., p. 15.

theatre had become 'weitgehend ein Museum ... in welchem die Kunstschätze alter Theaterepochen gezeigt werden'. It was saved — from the box-office point of view — by convention, by the oft-repeated and always believed opinion that classical plays must be good; they were a 'Goldwährung in der Kultur', certain of an audience, sure of applause, so that some actors had a fixed status, rather like Civil Servants and doctors.

The modern theatre can offer a very varied repertoire, as each epoch has developed its own particular style, but for the modern playwright style had become a personal thing:

'... eine Entscheidung von Fall zu Fall ... es gibt keinen Stil mehr, nur noch Stile ... gibt es nur noch Stile, gibt es nur noch Dramaturgien und keine Dramaturgie mehr: die Dramaturgie Brechts, die Dramaturgie Eliots, jene Claudels, jene Frischs, jene Hochwälders, eine Dramaturgie von Fall zu Fall.'[1]

If all these had to be comprised under one heading it would be that of 'eine Dramaturgie des Experiments', which would seek to investigate all the possibilities of the stage. This is precisely what Dürrenmatt and others to whom he is indebted (Wilder, Brecht, Claudel, Pirandello) have been trying to do.

What experiments are being made? Some, of special interest to Dürrenmatt, hinge on the relative importance assigned to the décor on the one hand, and the spoken

[1] *Theaterprobleme*, p. 21. '... a decision depending on individual cases ... there is no longer any style, only styles ... if there are only different styles, there are only dramatic theories and not *a* dramatic theory: one for Brecht, one for Eliot, one for Claudel, one for Frisch, one for Hochwälder ... a dramatic theory from one case to the next.'

word on the other. In many plays speech is assuming greater importance and to some extent replacing the theatrical setting, whilst in others the place of action is becoming more abstract or generalized, or there may be a combination of both these factors. One example of this has already been mentioned: Wilder's *Our Town*, where the stage is empty except for the barest necessities — tables, chairs, or ladders — and the spoken word, the imagination of the audience, and the miming of the players help to complete the picture of the small town. This is 'Entstofflichung' (dematerialization or disillusionment) of the setting, which 'alienates' the audience, that is, makes them less emotionally involved in the scene before them. The second and perhaps more important example of 'Entstofflichung' is when it is applied to the place of action, as in Wilder's *The Skin of our Teeth*, where we never find out exactly where the Anthropus family live, beyond that, for instance, it is during a war or in the Ice Age. The effect of these two devices is to focus the attention of the audience on to the characters and also, where the locality becomes purposely abstract, to make it clear that the action and the problems posed apply to mankind as a whole. In other words the stage, with less elaborate décor, is widening its scope. Other examples of this vagueness of locality are frequent enough in modern plays: no one knows where exactly Frisch's mysterious Graf Öderland acts his part or where the tramps wait for Godot. Dürrenmatt is far from explicit in the location of *Die Ehe des Herrn Mississippi*, whilst the stage directions in *Ein Engel kommt nach Babylon* make it clear that the action takes place in any big city.

'Entstofflichung' of the setting and place of action is only one aspect of Dürrenmatt's use of the stage: another important aim was to supplement and in some cases even to supersede the use of the spoken word. One thinks immediately of the increasing disintegration of the room in *Die Ehe des Herrn Mississippi*, the nebula of Andromeda projecting itself on to the stage in *Ein Engel kommt nach Babylon*, and the progress from ramshackle dilapidation to brash, spick-and-span modernity in *Der Besuch der alten Dame*. In each case the visual impression tells us forcefully, and sometimes also symbolically, what course the action is taking. What fascinated Dürrenmatt in this connection was

'... daß mit der Bühne gedichtet wird ... eine Möglichkeit, die mich seit jeher beschäftigt und die einer der Gründe, wenn nicht der Hauptgrund ist, warum ich Theaterstücke schreibe.'[1]

This desire to make the maximum use of the stage, to portray the world in its rich variety, leads often to confusion and misunderstanding:

'So wird mein Theater oft vieldeutig und scheint zu verworren. Auch schleichen sich Mißverständnisse ein, indem man verzweifelt im Hühnerstall meiner Dramen nach dem Ei der Erklärung sucht, das zu legen ich beharrlich mich weigere.'[2]

---

[1] *Theaterprobleme*, p. 25. '... that one should express creatively by means of the stage ... a possibility which has always occupied my attention and which is one of the reasons, if not the main reason, why I write plays.'

[2] Ibid., p. 29. 'So my theatre becomes ambiguous and seems too confused. Misunderstandings also creep in, when people search desperately in the hen-house of my dramas for the egg of explanation, which I obstinately refuse to lay.'

If we remember also that Dürrenmatt frequently gives a very free rein to his imagination, this will help in obtaining a correct assessment of his work.

In the latter half of his essay, Dürrenmatt explains why he thinks that our modern world offers little scope for tragedy. Schiller's approach to the problem, with its assumption of a fixed moral order against which all earthly striving could be measured, is no longer valid. The world he wrote of was reflected in the world around him. This basis for tragedy is no longer available: we have no more Wallensteins and the last tragic hero in the former sense of the term was Napoleon; we are left only with tragedies:

'... weil wir keine tragischen Helden, sondern nur Tragödien vorfinden, die von Weltmetzgern inszeniert und von Hackmaschinen ausgeführt werden. Aus Hitler und Stalin lassen sich keine Wallensteine machen — sie selber sind nur noch zufällige äußere Ausdrucksformen dieser Macht.'[1]

Power today can be compared to an iceberg — most of it lies below the surface — and for purposes of dramatic art remains anonymous and abstract. The only subjects for the dramatist are the victims of power, not those wielding it, who have little control over it and hardly know how they have acquired it. Tragedy demands, above all, guilt and responsibility, but in the hotchpotch of modern politics these are hard to find:

[1] Ibid., p. 44. '... because we find no tragic heroes, but only tragedies, which are produced by "world butchers" and carried out by mincing-machines. Hitler and Stalin can never be made into Wallensteins — they themselves are only the accidental outward expressions of this power.'

'... in der Wurstelei unseres Jahrhunderts, in diesem Kehraus der weißen Rasse, gibt es keine Schuldigen und auch keine Verantwortlichen mehr. Alle können nicht dafür und haben es nicht gewollt. Es geht wirklich ohne jeden. Alles wird mitgerissen und bleibt in irgend einem Rechen hängen. Wir sind zu kollektiv schuldig, zu kollektiv gebettet in die Sünden unserer Väter und Vorväter.'[1]

This is our bad luck, and all we can do is to approach it from the point of view of comedy, from the grotesque and the paradoxical. Tragedy as such is impossible, but we can come near to it in our comedies 'als einen schrecklichen Moment, als einen sich öffnenden Abgrund' ('as a terrible moment, as an abyss which suddenly yawns open').

Developing the theme of comedy, Dürrenmatt comes near to laying 'das Ei der Erklärung', which would elucidate some of the thought behind his works:

'Nun liegt der Schluß nahe, die Komödie sei der Ausdruck der Verzweiflung, doch ist dieser Schluß nicht zwingend. Wer das Sinnlose, das Hoffnungslose dieser Welt sieht, kann verzweifeln, doch ist diese Verzweiflung nicht eine Folge dieser Welt, sondern eine Antwort, die er auf diese Welt gibt, und eine andere Antwort wäre sein Nichtverzweifeln, sein Entschluß etwa, diese Welt zu bestehen, in der wir oft leben wie Gulliver unter den

---

[1] *Theaterprobleme*, p. 47. 'In the hotchpotch of our century, in this finish of the white race, no one bears the guilt and no one the responsibility. All people cannot help it and all have not wanted it. It just happens without anyone being responsible. Everyone gets dragged along with the current and is caught up in some grating or other. We are too collectively guilty, too collectively bedded in the sins of our fathers and forefathers.'

Riesen. Auch der nimmt Distanz, auch der tritt einen Schritt zurück, der seinen Gegner einschätzen will, der sich bereit macht, mit ihm zu kämpfen oder ihm zu entgehen. Es ist immer noch möglich, den mutigen Menschen zu zeigen. Dies ist denn auch eines meiner Hauptanliegen.'[1]

Comedy, by creating distance, enables the writer to step back, survey the world, and seek an answer to its problems, especially in the figure of the courageous person. The blind duke, Romulus (*Romulus der Grosse*), Übelohe (*Die Ehe des Herrn Mississippi*), and Akki (*Ein Engel kommt nach Babylon*) are all cast in this pattern: in a world where moral order and established values have given way to vice and corruption, in a world on the brink of disaster, such people do not despair, but take a step backwards to take the measure of their opponents, and the lost moral order is restored in their hearts. There must be no capitulation to this monster of a world: this is the positive message that rings through many of Dürrenmatt's plays. To disseminate this message to an ever-widening public, the playwright must not only have recourse to comedy, but also be prepared, by his inventiveness and originality — 'der Einfall' is the term used — to trick the public into listening

[1] Ibid., p. 49. 'From this one might conclude that comedy is the expression of despair, but this conclusion does not have to be accepted. Whoever sees the senselessness, the hopelessness, of this world can despair, yet this despair is not a consequence of this world, but an answer which one gives to this world, and another answer would be not to despair, but to decide, perhaps, to stand up against this world, in which we often live like Gulliver amongst the giants. He too goes back some distance, he too takes a step backwards, who wants to weigh up his adversary, who is preparing to fight with him or escape from him. It is still possible to show the courageous man. This, too, is one of my main preoccupations.'

to ideas which in other backgrounds would not interest them: 'Die Komödie ist eine Mausefalle in die das Publikum immer wieder geriet und immer wieder geraten wird.'[1] ('Comedy is a mousetrap in which the public has been caught again and again and in which it will always get caught.')

To capture or fascinate the public in this manner demands from the writer a personal, original, and inventive approach towards all aspects of his work: plot, dialogue, characters, and stagecraft in particular. Dürrenmatt has this in rich measure and it is this, rather than any doctrines which he may or may not propound, which stamps him as a great artist. His is the original, personal approach, which precedes any consideration of dramatic rules:

'So ist es denn mein Weg, dem zu mißtrauen, was man den Bau des Dramas nennt, und ihn vom Besonderen, vom Einfall her zu erreichen suchen, und nicht vom Allgemeinen, vom Plane her.'[2]

Dürrenmatt's ingenious choice and use of material are reflected in the range and great individuality of his work. Not only is each plot, each setting, highly original — one might even say unique — but almost every page gives evidence of a skilful use of dialogue and situation to produce the maximum theatrical effect. His latest play *Der Meteor* (1966) is perhaps the best in this respect. This talent has earned for him the title of 'die stärkste Potenz des deutsch-sprechenden Theaters'.

A concomitant, if not a prerequisite, of originality, of

---

[1] *Theaterprobleme*, p. 50.
[2] Ibid., p. 52. 'So it is my method to mistrust what is called the structure of the drama and instead to build on particular ideas and original approaches and not on a general plan.'

the inventive mind, is that the writer must be prepared to let himself go, to follow the whims of his art: 'Es besteht für mich die Nötigung, ins Blaue hineinzuschreiben.' A good example of this 'letting one's hair down' is in *Grieche sucht Griechin*, when Antiolochus runs amok after discovering the truth of his position. Here Dürrenmatt shows his flair for using impulsive writing without letting it get too much out of hand, though he does admit:

'Dialoge können verführen, Wortspiele, die einen unvermutet vom Stoff wegtreiben. Doch gibt es immer wieder Einfälle, denen man nicht wiederstehen darf, ... neben der Vorsicht, den Einfällen zu widerstehen, muß auch der Mut vorhanden sein, sich ihnen auszusetzen.'[1]

Another reason why comedy is preferred, apart from the lack of new tragic characters, is that the old ones such as Caesar have been so dissected and analysed by historians and others that the tragedian has little left to say. He can either revert to obscurer figures and make a comedy of them, or make a parody of the so-called great personalities. This latter method is employed with considerable success in *Romulus der Große*. When the great are parodied, a picture is made of them which is in contrast to what they were, so that they are made to look ridiculous or even grotesque. This act of parody gives the writer back the freedom he has lost because of the dearth of genuine tragic figures:

[1] Ibid., p. 37. 'Dialogues can lead astray [and become] a play upon words, which unexpectedly drives one away from one's subject-matter. But there are always ideas which one must not resist, ... as well as caution in resisting ideas, there must always be present the courage to lay oneself open to them.'

'Durch diesen Akt der Parodie gewinnt der Dichter seine Freiheit und damit den Stoff, der nicht mehr zu finden, sondern nur noch zu erfinden ist, denn jede Parodie setzt ein Erfinden voraus. Die Dramaturgie der vorhandenen Stoffe wird durch die Dramaturgie der erfundenen Stoffe abgelöst.'[1]

Laughing is the only means we have of showing our freedom, and ridicule is the only weapon feared by the tyrants of this planet. For this reason our literature has been invaded by parody, ridicule, satire, and the grotesque. Even so, most people ignore these as soon as they are made uncomfortable by them:

'Doch in dem Moment, wo das Komische als das Gefährliche, Aufdeckende, Fordernde, Moralische erkannt wird, läßt man es fahren wie ein heißes Eisen, denn die Kunst darf alles sein, wenn sie nur gemütlich bleibt.'[2]

'Gemütlichkeit' is not enough for Dürrenmatt, however. He cannot retire into an ivory tower, but feels it is his duty to warn mankind of the way it is going:

'Die heutige Menschheit gleicht einer Autofahrerin. Sie fährt immer schneller, immer rücksichtsloser ihre Straße. Doch hat sie es nicht gern, wenn der konsternierte

---

[1] *Theaterprobleme*, p. 55. 'By this act of parody the poet wins his freedom and therefore his subject-matter, which he has now not to find, but only to invent, for every parody presupposes an invention. The dramaturgy of available subject-matter is replaced by the dramaturgy of invented subject-matter.'

[2] Ibid., p. 56. 'But at the moment when the comical is recognized as dangerous, revealing, demanding, or moralizing, it is dropped like a hot brick, for art may be everything it wants to be, provided it keeps to what is "comfortable".'

Mitfahrer "Achtung" schreit, und "Hier ist eine Warnungstafel".'[1]

The poet of today cannot devote himself exclusively to the aesthetic demands of his craft, but is forced by the folly and excesses of his fellow-men to point out the dangerous situation in which they find themselves: 'die Angst, die Sorge und vor allem der Zorn reißt seinen Mund auf.'[2]

Dürrenmatt gives in conclusion his views on the prospects of the theatre and the playwright. If it is not to stagnate, the theatre must offer scope to the author who wishes to experiment, but this is becoming increasingly difficult, because of the preference given to the museum-type, classical production, with its respectable box-office appeal. We are living on the cultural capital of the past; so much so, that the modern playwright is lucky if he can have more than a single performance to try out his ideas, whilst being hounded by critics, who expect from him the perfection the classics are supposed to have. If this process continues, there will be an abundance of critics, but no creative writers. He ends by suggesting that the only course left open to the creative writer is to write crime stories, which are beneath the contempt of critics.

Romulus der Große

This play was first performed at Basle in 1949. Though his most successful play to date, Dürrenmatt revised it, making considerable changes to the last act, which in the

[1] Ibid., p. 57. 'Mankind today resembles a motorist who goes on his way ever more quickly, ever more inconsiderately, but doesn't like it when his dumbfounded fellow-traveller shouts "Look out!" and "Here is a warning sign!"'

[2] Ibid., p. 57. '... fear, worry, and especially anger forces him to open his mouth.'

1957 version gives more stature to the figure of **Romulus**. This experimenting with the stage and the change-over to comedy after the seriousness of his first two plays is in keeping with the ideas expressed in *Theaterprobleme*. Furthermore, the comic vein is completely in accordance with Dürrenmatt's own temperament, as we are assured by Elisabeth Brock-Sulzer:

'Die Komödie ist für Dürrenmatt nicht nur eine Waffe des Angriffs. Sie ist auch das, was sie von Natur aus ist, ein Ausdruck des Lachens, eine Frucht der Heiterkeit. Denn Dürrenmatt hat das Pech, bei voller Einsicht in unsere heutige, totale Gefährdung, ein lustiger, zur Heiterkeit bestimmter Mensch zu sein. Er ist weder moros noch trüb, er lebt voll und gern. Er liebt die saftigen, prallen Geschichten, er ist einer der wenigen, echten Fabulierer unten den heutigen Dichtern.'[1]

Ample evidence of the truth of this assertion is given in *Romulus der Große*.

The general setting is similar to the background of his first two plays. Like Hebbel, Dürrenmatt seeks dramatic effect in a turning-point in history, when the established order is being threatened on all sides by disintegrating forces. The action takes place during the break-up of the western Roman Empire, under its last ruler Romulus, at the hands of the Germanic invaders, led by Odoaker.

---

[1] 'The comedy is for Dürrenmatt not only a weapon of attack. It is also what it is by its very nature, an expression of laughing, a fruit of cheerfulness. For Dürrenmatt has the bad luck to have a full insight into the extremely dangerous position of the world today and at the same time to be a merry, cheerful man. He is neither morose nor gloomy: he enjoys life to the full. He loves ripe, juicy stories. He is one of the few genuine story-tellers amongst the writers of today.'
Friedrich Dürrenmatt: Stationen seines Werkes, p. 30.

INTRODUCTION

The date has been altered to the Ides of March, A.D. 476, to fit in with the parody on Caesar's death in Act Three. This concentrated piece of comedy illustrates Dürrenmatt's views that historic figures should be brought down to size ('reduziert') and their so-called greatness exposed for what it is. Caesar, and by implication all military leaders, are made to look ridiculous by the actions and opinions of Romulus, who debunks established conceptions of the greatness of the Roman Empire and puts in a firm plea for the overriding importance of human values. He starts as a comical, almost burlesque figure, but attains stature and dignity as the play proceeds. The Empire he insists on forfeiting is a symbol of the decline in Western civilization and culture, the sell-out of the latter being pointedly portrayed in his dealings with Apollyon, the art dealer, who buys from him busts of the Roman emperors and poets. The ruler's calm indifference in the face of impending doom contrasts sharply with the panic measures taken by those around him, and offers ample scope for comedy of the Dürrenmatt type, which is often based on the debunking or the discomfiture of individual characters.

Big business is parodied in Cäsar Rupf (*rupfen* = to fleece), a trouser-manufacturer, who is willing to save the Empire with his millions, if he can marry Rea, the Emperor's daughter — a somewhat melodramatic plan brought in for comical effect. His suggestion, received with general acclamation, leaves the Emperor cold. This refusal is the first hint of Romulus's true character, his basic humanity and his common-sense approach towards the problems of life. Till this moment he has been something of a buffoon, with a passion for poultry-rearing and great concern for his own comfort. The first act finishes with a general verdict on Romulus: 'Rom hat einen schändlichen Kaiser!' This anticipates the final words of the second act, which again sum up the course of the action: 'Dieser Kaiser muß weg!'

These words are spoken by Ämilian, betrothed to Rea; he returns from captivity so mutilated that he can only be recognized by his ring, an obvious reference to the atrocities of the last war. In the postscript Dürrenmatt calls him 'die Gegengestalt zu Romulus, ... das tausendfach besudelte Opfer der Macht'. He is the type who will go on fighting even when conditions are hopeless and the cause uncertain; though courageous and of undoubted integrity, he is easily induced to make enormous sacrifices for an institution such as the Empire, which, in Romulus's view, is not worth it. He is not far removed from Shakespeare's soldier 'seeking the bubble reputation even in the cannon's mouth'. By his blind belief in patriotic clichés he helps in the continuance of war, even whilst falling a victim to it. By his wounds, however, and his words, he is a condemnation of its bestiality, a prey to the system and military leaders such as da Ponte and Theoderich, Odoaker's ambitious nephew.

Ämilian's appearance, disfigured, pale, and gaunt, at the dilapidated imperial villa, his dazed 'Die Villa des Kaisers in Campanien?', make a truly tragic impression and the sequence of the action focused on him forms one of the 'Abgründe der Tragik', the terrible moments which can occur in comedy. The genuineness of the tragic in Ämilian's position is heightened by the contrast with the hollow-sounding classical verses recited by Rea, but alleviated by the frequent interspersion of comical incidents. If the action becomes dramatic or serious, it is rudely interrupted by the loud cackling of Romulus's hens, all named after emperors. Whenever Zeno, the Eastern Emperor, tries to become pontifical, he finds he has stepped on to an egg hidden in the weeds. By this skilful blending of differing effects Dürrenmatt is using the stage as an instrument on which he plays.

Act Three, theatrically the most effective, is a parody on the murder of Julius Caesar, with the inevitable twist at the end. All want to flee, but Romulus, assuming greater dignity as the play progresses, chooses to stay, revealing that he only accepted the title because he wanted to put an end to the Empire, which is 'eine Einrichtung, die öffentlich Mord, Plünderung, Unterdrückung und Brandschatzung auf Kosten der andern Völker betrieb. . . .' Whilst drinking with Ämilian, he treads on the fingers of the 'Innenminister', Tulius Rotundus, who is under the bed. The remaining would-be assassins, who include most of the secondary characters, either drop out of wall-cupboards or creep from under the bed, all in dark cloaks. Romulus is completely unperturbed; only when the cook appears is he visibly shaken and utters the well-known words, suitably amended: 'Koch, auch du? Und mit dem Messer, womit du so unzählige Kaiser ermordet hast?' The speech which follows, long and moralizing, is in sharp contrast to the burlesque situation: Romulus condemns the Roman Empire for its inhumanity, cruelty and greed. He towers morally over his attackers and looks down on them in the majesty of his great humanity, defying these slaves of the orthodox mentality, whose attitude and lack of courage is responsible for much of the world's misery. The message applies as much to Western civilization as to Rome. The act finishes with a typical

Dürrenmatt twist when the cry 'Die Germanen kommen!' forces all to flee except Romulus and the weary Spurius Titus Mamma, who is snoring on the bed.

Dürrenmatt had said that it was his intention to reverse the usual course of a tragedy, where the hero succumbs to the forces of history, in order to let history die at the hands of the hero. Such is Romulus's hope as the third act ends, but once again the forces of reality prove superior to human desires and efforts.

The final act, again completely paradoxical, shows the meeting next morning between Romulus and Odoaker, the Germanic leader. The first surprise comes when he offers his submission to Romulus, whose wisdom, justice, and humanity he admires greatly and which constitute for him true greatness, as opposed to the spurious, militant greatness of his nephew Theoderich. Romulus, in the opinion of Odoaker, is the only man fit to govern the world: if he does not accept this responsibility, Theoderich will build a second empire, worse and more bestial than ever the Roman was. They agree that there is no way out, that reality, in the form of inhumanity and lust for power, conquers all efforts towards a more humane government on this planet. Even if Theoderich were killed, new tyrants would arise. Odoaker finally agrees to let Romulus go into retirement, for all they can hope to do is to stave off disaster for a few years. Their resignation is expressed in the two statements, 'Wir sind in einem Teufelskreis gefangen' and 'Die Wirklichkeit hat unsere Ideen korrigiert!' The Empire is officially dissolved, Odoaker is made King of Italy, and Romulus goes into retirement.

The play is basically a plea for humanity and an attack against militarism, power politics, and the stupidity of government. Romulus is the ideal character to lead this attack: humane, but also ruthless and ready to make the final sacrifice for his ideals. His tragedy lies in the comedy of his retirement and his greatness in his graceful acceptance of this, for the final message is completely objective and tinged with melancholy: 'Tun wir so,' says Romulus, '... als siegte der Geist über die Materie Mensch.' ('Let us act, ... as if the spirit were conquering man, the material.') Though both Romulus and Odoaker are examples of Dürrenmatt's courageous man, they are far from faultless, in that they have had no regard for the all-important present: Romulus wanted only to destroy the past, whilst Odoaker was concerned with the future:

'Wir ließen uns von zwei Gespenstern bestimmen, denn wir haben keine Macht über das, was war and über das, was sein wird. Macht haben wir nur über die Gegenwart, an die wir nicht gedacht haben und an der wir nun beide scheitern.'[1]

Here we hear the down-to-earth Swiss speaking, with both feet planted firmly on the ground, the heir to Keller and Gotthelf.

The situation at the end of the comedy is similar to that at the conclusion of *Die Physiker*. A group of men trying to save mankind from disaster find themselves submerged in the tide of events around them; all their scheming is frustrated by reality and indeed renders the impending holocaust all the more certain; because of human failings

[1] 'We let our actions be determined by two ghosts, for we have no power over that which was and that which is in the future. We have only power over the present, about which we didn't think and which now ruins us both.'

— 'die Materie Mensch' — tyranny and war are a permanent feature of life on this planet.

Die Ehe des Herrn Mississippi

Die Ehe des Herrn Mississippi, Dürrenmatt's next play (1952), makes very efficient use of a restricted setting and is a good example of Dürrenmatt's objective, 'mit der Bühne dichten'. All the action is round a 'Biedermeiertischchen' in Mississippi's house, and the gradual disintegration of the room is a sign of the path to ruin taken by the characters and a symbol of the increasing moral and spiritual bankruptcy of Western civilization. Reference has already been made to Dürrenmatt's interest in painting and sketching, which gave him a keen appreciation of the visual impression made by his writings. Though following after *Romulus der Große*, this 'comedy in two parts' stands closer to the two earlier plays. Surrealistic and impressionistic touches, with an extravagant use of ingenious theatrical devices, combine to produce a panoramic effect and an atmosphere of decay and devastation such as prevailed in *Der Blinde* and *Es steht geschrieben*. Apart from the fact that all the action takes place in one room, the play is most unclassical in its eccentricities and excesses; it stands in sharp contrast to *Die Physiker*, Dürrenmatt's most classical play.

The rapid pace of action owes much to Anastasia, the only woman, whose poisoning of her husband enables Mississippi, the State Prosecutor, to force her to marry him. Mississippi, a rigid moralist and devotee of the laws of Moses, has poisoned his own wife for adultery with the husband of Anastasia, but the latter's motive was an attachment for the idealistic Graf Bodo Übelohe, who unwittingly supplies the poison in each case. This very ingenious plot, reminiscent of a detective story, is unfolded in the opening scene between Anastasia and Mississippi. It is soon evident that he represents an attitude of mind in its most extreme form rather than a fully rounded flesh-and-blood personality. Such characters make it difficult for one to agree with Dürrenmatt's statement that his plays are first and foremost about persons.

Anastasia, too, is more than flesh and blood: she has been called by Bänziger 'eine Männerfresserin und Giftmischerin', who has 'einen ungeheueren Männerverbrauch'.[1] She symbolizes the will to enjoy life to the full and is so unscrupulous that even in the throes of death she persists in lying assertions of her own innocence. As the crisis becomes more acute, she uses her charms to bewitch all the main characters in the hope of escaping from the imminent disaster. Her opportunism is matched only by that of the Minister Diego, a type often found in Dürrenmatt's plays. The dramatic action, already tensed, is finally triggered off by the remaining two participants, both representing extremes of personality: St. Claude, who has the secret of Mississippi's very murky past, is a revolutionary of the Left, completely ruthless in his unrelenting search for social justice; Übelohe, the character nearest to Dürrenmatt's heart, is an idealist, cast in the mould of Albert Schweitzer, who sacrifices everything in his zeal to help humanity, but is for ever dogged by misfortune and ill health. He is a glorious failure, but also another of Dürrenmatt's courageous men.

The persons whom fate thrusts together round the coffee-table in the Mississippi–Anastasia household repre-

[1] *Frisch und Dürrenmatt*, Francke Verlag, Bern, 1960, pp. 146, 147.

sent extrapolations of types rather than ordinary people: by their very intensity and lack of compromise they create a vortex which whirls most of them to their doom, in a manner not unreminiscent of Kleist, for whom Dürrenmatt had a very high regard. The implication, often asserted by Dürrenmatt, is that drastic individual efforts to solve humanity's problems are foredoomed to failure; much to be preferred are minor but consistent contributions from the mass of the people.

Following a film technique, the play begins and ends with the shooting of St. Claude by political fanatics. Instead of dying, he turns round and addresses the audience, telling them that the next scene happened five years ago and introducing the main characters. As the events extend over such a long period, these and other devices are used to give the play the necessary epic breadth and rapid development of action. The factual and critical addresses to the audience are illustrated by the raising or lowering of back-cloths, and appropriate sound-effects. This 'Entstofflichung' of the stage aims at destroying the illusion that what is represented is 'real' in any but an artistic sense. This effect is also assisted by the purposely vague setting: the scene from one window shows a southern landscape, with cypress trees and an ancient ruined temple, whereas the other reveals a northern town with a Gothic cathedral. Although we are in the first storey, characters or crowds flit past the windows as the occasion demands, or enter through the window or the grandfather clock; the inevitable statue of Eros serves as a coat-hanger. In much of this the influence of Wilder and Brecht is obvious, whilst the abstract setting is frequently found in modern plays.

With these resources, the action acquires a rapid momentum, which exaggerates the excesses and intensity of the main characters. Long after his marriage to Anastasia, Mississippi's seemingly stable world is twice shaken to the foundations within a matter of minutes by a double-pronged attack from Diego, the opportunist Minister and typical 'Konjunkturritter', and the Communist St. Claude: the former tells him he must resign owing to public nausea over his spate of executions, the latter threatens to besmirch his reputation unless he offers to support the revolution. He rejects outright both suggestions, even though St. Claude threatens to stir up the people against him.

In what follows, three different methods of communication are used simultaneously, so that the action, more epic than dramatic, surges forward at breakneck speed. The huge back-cloth is explained in turn by Übelohe and Mississippi: St. Claude has exposed the State Prosecutor, banners stating 'Tod dem Massenmörder' float past the upper-storey window of the house, which has been stoned and damaged. Anastasia is being threatened by Mississippi and Übelohe, who want her to confess her sins; Mississippi is under political pressure from Diego and St. Claude. The Lulu-like Anastasia — not unreminiscent of Wedekind — uses her charms on each of the others in an effort to escape with the one who would offer her most. The action, fully charged with the inflexibility and intenseness of the characters, presses forward with dynamic impetus. Übelohe seems to be speaking for all and for mankind as a whole when he refers to 'diese zusammensinkende Welt unserer Sünden'.

Though there are numerous comical touches, the general

impression gained is that of the grotesque: one feels that figures from Hieronymus Bosch or even Georg Groß have been brought to life. This grotesque view of the world is meant by Dürrenmatt to contrast with the world as God intended it, and as such is a searing criticism of our times. The use of the grotesque is a basic feature of Dürrenmatt's drama; here individual features are harshly exaggerated and the interplay of intense emotions produces a rasping effect which is even more accentuated by the apocalyptic thrust of the action. The characters perhaps deserve their doom, but it is in any case inevitable. We feel that a judgement is being made on the Western world's declining standards of culture and morality, or even that the whole purpose of existence is being questioned. This impression, confirmed by the abstract setting, gives the action a universal validity reminiscent of Ionesco, Beckett, and other dramatists of the Theatre of the Absurd.

The second part shows an increase in the pace of the action and in the use of violence. St. Claude and the Minister stand in turn at the window; as red banners float past, the Communist tells of the revolt he has started; encouraged by the clappings of an invisible crowd, Diego finds the situation ideal for a seizure of power. Übelohe, completely drunk, awaits the return of Mississippi, who is chased in by the mob, tattered and torn, battered and bleeding. The ensuing conversation between the two under the small table, as salvos crash into the room, is one of those incongruous situations often introduced by Dürrenmatt when the action might tend to flag. This scene forms the highlight of the play, especially when reinforced by the appearance, through doors, windows, and the grandfather clock, of numerous white-clad doctors in thick horn-rimmed glasses: Mississippi is to be taken to the lunatic asylum. Even in his inebriated condition, the Count's pronouncements reflect Dürrenmatt's views on the inevitable march of reality, the individual's relative impotence, and the need for justice and truth. Both he and Mississippi have failed in their efforts to help humanity, just as Romulus and the physicists fail.

The continuity and impetus of the action are maintained by St. Claude, who tells the audience of his own fall and the Minister's rise to power. Subsequent events in the room — now reduced to rubble — take on a somewhat melodramatic turn. Mississippi, still frantically seeking the truth about his wife, escapes from the asylum and poisons her, but himself takes the poison she has intended for St. Claude, who is then shot by three men in raincoats — a re-enactment of the first scene. The play concludes with a parody of the Greek chorus, the characters expressing to the audience their views on life and the parts they have played: the Minister, desiring nothing but power and lacking in all ideals, has conquered the world; Anastasia cannot change her sensual, materialist nature, even when dying; Mississippi and St. Claude represent the ruthless and misguided idealists, who return to the world in ever-changing forms, bringing with them death and destruction:

MISSISSIPPI: Fegen wir hin über eure Städte.
ST. CLAUDE: Drehen wir keuchend die mächtigen Flügel.
MISSISSIPPI: Die Mühle treibend, die euch zermalmt.

The last word is left to the courageous man, who wages an unceasing but also unavailing battle on behalf of the common man, the victim of power-seekers: Übelohe appears as a battered Don Quixote in the shadow of the flailing windmill vanes and offers defiance to the blind forces crushing mankind, even though he knows his struggle to be hopeless and ridiculous. This final speech makes Übelohe a kinsman of the blind duke, Romulus, and Akki.

In this play we have a dramatic interpretation, probably better than in any other by Dürrenmatt, of the critical situation in the world today and the forces responsible for this. Dürrenmatt's grotesque world, stridently assertive, is a paradoxical plea for a return to the transcendental values inherent in Schiller. Mankind is basically materialist and sadly lacking in the true spiritual values which alone ward off disaster. The St. Claudes and the Mississippis, with their radical, ruthless, Hitlerian approach, increase human misery but achieve nothing. The Übelohes may have the answer to our problems, but are swamped by the tide of reality, which is carried forward by human ignorance and impetuosity, but above all by the irrationality of events.

Die Ehe des Herrn Mississippi, though entitled a comedy, is the most 'ungemütlich' of Dürrenmatt's plays and reflects many of the doctrines put forward in *Theaterprobleme*. An insight into the nature of his experimenting is afforded by a study of the first version, particularly the stage direction that the setting was to be 'reichlich irrsinnig, als befände man sich unten in einem Höllentrichter, als wäre der Raum oben für Riesen und unten für Zwerge gebaut'. In the final version this is summed up in the sentence 'Der Raum stinkt zum Himmel'. We are to see a picture of human depravity, lying, and selfishness, in a world without any stable social order, where spiritual and cultural values are riddled with materialism or hedonism. This is confirmed by the disparate views from the windows — neatly named by Bänziger 'tote Kulturlandschaft' — and the relics of past centuries which furnish the room. Everything is aimed at achieving an apocalyptic effect: the breath-taking sweep of the action; surrealistic Kafkaesque features, intermingled with touches of the grotesque; the biting, rasping dialogue, watered down for the second version, but still scathing in its implications; most significant of all, the *outré* characters, whose fiery interaction upon one another, fanned by Anastasia's devilish attractions, creates the frenzy of passions which finally seals their fate and symbolizes the decadence and disintegration of modern society.

The keyword for the play is exaggeration: not only in characterization and dialogue, but in the use of every possible theatrical device to produce the effect of a hollow-based society hurtling towards destruction. In some ways the play is an inversion of Schiller's approach, which entailed the selection of exaggerated characters to portray moral greatness.

Ein Engel kommt nach Babylon

The violence and harsh overtones of *Die Ehe des Herrn Mississippi* are almost completely lacking in *Ein Engel kommt nach Babylon*, which has some of the magic simplicity of the fairy-tale, together with the ready wit and gaiety of the 'Wiener Volkstheater' of Raimund and Nestroy. The décor is abstract and generalized — 'ein Phantasie-Babylon' — with modern features: skyscrapers, lamp-posts, and so on; it is a parody of any modern city and the issues involved apply also to modern times. The appearance of the angel enables Dürrenmatt, the keen student of astronomy, to give an outer-space view of the earth, its beauty, splendour, and infinite variety, misused by man in his ignorance and exploited by power-seekers. Against these the courageous man, Akki the beggar, wages a relentless but vain struggle. On him has fallen the mantle of Graf Bodo Übelohe, and Romulus.

The plot of this fragmentary comedy in three acts is highly original in conception and development. At the opening an angel, disguised as a beggar, steps on to the Euphrates quay from the Andromeda nebula, which fills up half the background, bringing together in tangible form heaven and earth, the source and scene of the action. The angel, a humorous figure with Mephistophelean traits, escorts the beautiful girl Kurrubi, God's gift to mankind, who is to marry the poorest man on earth, Akki the beggar. King Nebuchadnezzar, a would-be social reformer, is disguised as a beggar in an effort to persuade Akki to give up his calling, so a begging contest is held to find out who is to win Kurrubi's hand. In a scene rich in humour, satire, and comical incidents, Akki easily defeats the king, who is now the poorest beggar and claimed by Kurrubi. The competition, probably the best scene in the play, introduces a gay assortment of rather burlesque characters: tile workers going on the early-morning shift, and Gimmil, the 'Eselmilchverkäufer', with his slogan 'Babylonische Patrioten trinken Eselmilch!' The inclusion of Enggibi, the local financial wizard, Tabtum, a fiery-tempered courtesan, and the king's soldiers gives a fair cross-section of the community, whose reaction to the arrival of the heavenly maiden forms an integral part of the play.

In the second act, under the Euphrates bridge, we meet Akki at home, surrounded by the acquisitions of his trade:

'Sarkophage, Negergötzen, alte Königsthrone, babylonische Fahrräder und Autopneus. . . .' Like the ruins of Mississippi's room and the Emperor's tumbledown villa, this junk-yard symbolizes the decay of our modern civilization and culture. Such settings also offer easy access to comedy and satire: the characters in Romulus tread on eggs at inopportune moments; Mississippi, unabashed in spite of detonations, moralizes under the table. The technique achieves maximum comical and satirical effect in the figure of Hercules, wallowing in the foul-smelling quagmire which has deluged the Augean king's domain (*Herkules und der Stall des Augias*).

The beggar's free-and-easy character, his scorn for wealth and authority, are soon revealed: he throws jewellery into the river and the inevitable statue of Eros on to the debris. Nothing said creates a serious impression: the atmosphere is that of a fairy-tale, interspersed with scenes from a cartoon or burlesque comedy. This air of complete unconcernedness gives the play its peculiar charm. Even the appearance of the hangman leaves Akki completely unmoved: he always has the situation well in hand and finally obtains for himself the position of hangman. He symbolizes the Arab love of story-telling and entertains the assembled poets, whose patron he is, with the 'Makame' of his life, told in short, rhymed prose, a form used by Arab narrators. His view of life is that only as a beggar can one survive the constant upheavals of history.

After this somewhat didactic interlude, different characters make attempts, in short doggerel verse, to woo Kurrubi. The appearance of the angel, settling on the head of the National Hero, causes a diversion and Kurrubi is led off to the king: 'Zum König mit dem Himmelsmädchen! ... Es soll unsere Königin sein!'

The final act is in Nebuchadnezzar's throne-room, the furnishings and decorations being a mixture of the greatest luxury and bestial gruesomeness, a symbol of the material plenty and moral emptiness of our age. The act has been criticized as being overladen and complicated, but this confusion reflects also the confusion of a community when exposed to temptation or asked to make sacrifices. In this respect it anticipates *Der Besuch der alten Dame*. Long discussions take place between the 'Obertheologe', the 'Erzminister', and the king in a vain effort to get Kurrubi to marry Nebuchadnezzar. The materialism and unscrupulous opportunism of the two high officials offer ample scope to Dürrenmatt's wit and satire. These are also given free rein — especially his scorn for nationalism and patriotic slogans — when the rioting populace break into the palace. Dürrenmatt's mordant criticism is aimed as much at the fickleness of the crowd as at the vices of authority. After another brief appearance of the angel, praising the wonders of the earth, Kurrubi is condemned as a witch, for no one is prepared to make the sacrifice of poverty to marry her. Akki is commissioned to kill her and bury her in the desert.

As we have seen in *Romulus*, characterization in Dürrenmatt is rather flimsy. In this case the king, hitherto an incompetent tyrant with a passion for hanging, displays unexpected wisdom by an admirable summing-up of the situation:

'Ich verriet das Mädchen um meiner Macht willen, der Minister verriet es der Staatskunst, der Priester der

Theologie zuliebe, ihr habt es um eurer Habe willen verraten.'

Akki's final 'Makame', as he escapes into the desert with Kurrubi, praises the beauty of the earth and the goodness of God, but points to the need for eternal striving. His basic optimism makes him a more positive character than Graf Bodo, whose concluding speech is very similar. In an explanatory note to the second version, Dürrenmatt fully supports the viewpoint of Akki and the angel:

'Immer noch hat der Engel recht, immer noch ist die Erde *das* Wunder. Der Engel mag uns weltfremd erscheinen, ich glaube jedoch daß jene weltfremder sind, welche die Welt nur als Verzweiflung sehen.'[1]

This is the message of the play: any State lacking in spiritual values, not appreciating God's grace and the inherent beauty of the earth, is destined for destruction; materialism, 'Realpolitik', and greed lead the people only to their doom.

The success of the comedy lies in a subtle and skilful blending of theatrical effectiveness, comedy, and satire, with an element of didacticism, in a happy-go-lucky, almost unreal atmosphere. Hangings, butchery, wars of conquest, human selfishness, and vanity are the order of the day, but no one, especially Akki, takes these seriously and we are certain that he will win through. This gives the play the aura of a fairy-tale with the expected happy ending, in spite of its sombre message. It is Dürrenmatt's answer to the absurdity of the world, 'Wenn man trotzdem

[1] 'The angel is still right: the earth is still *the* wonder. The angel may appear ignorant of the ways of the world, but I think they are even more so, who look upon the world with despair.'

lacht', and some light relief after the severity of *Mississippi*, just as Kleist's *Käthchen von Heilbronn* makes up for the excesses of *Penthesilea*.

Der Besuch der alten Dame

Der Besuch der alten Dame (1956), acclaimed by many as Dürrenmatt's masterpiece, has a straightforward, streamlined action. The obtrusive moralizings of earlier plays are omitted or only implied, whilst the characters, by Dürrenmatt's own confession, are ordinary, everyday people, not embodiments of some attitude of mind. There are points in common with *Ein Engel*: both plays deal with the reactions of a community to an extraordinary event, where self-interest conquers moral scruples; a supernatural happening sets the chain of action moving in *Ein Engel*, whilst Claire Zachanassian's offer to the town of Güllen[1] is nothing short of a miracle in the eyes of the penurious citizens. The town — 'das verärmteste, lausigste, erbärmlichste Nest der Strecke Venedig–Stockholm' — is ramshackle and nearly destitute, for the fabulously wealthy Claire, now in her sixties, has closed down all its industry, with the single-minded intention of obtaining justice from her one-time lover Ill, whose perjury has precipitated her into a life of vice. A victim of the wickedness of the world, she has come back to sit in judgement on it. She is a heartless, almost machine-like fury, but, with her wooden leg and ivory arm, not without a touch of the comical and grotesque, somewhat reminiscent of Kleist's Kunigunde in *Käthchen von Heilbronn*.

Her entourage is constituted so as to be theatrically effective — to give that touch of the incongruous so dear

[1] From *die Gülle*, liquid manure.

to Dürrenmatt — and to fill in the picture of her character. The two hostile witnesses at her trial are now the blind eunuchs Koby and Loby, an act of punishment carried out for her by Roby and Toby, ex-gangsters from Manhattan and the counterparts of the male nurses in *Die Physiker*. Her husbands numbers 7 and 8, as also the butler, formerly the judge at her trial, have names ending in '-oby'. This nomenclature expresses the dehumanization and depersonalization of her following: others are mere puppets; she manages them, the embodiment of an unfeeling, malignant fate, entirely lacking in human warmth and emotion, an ice-cold instrument of divine justice or devilish vengeance. This austerity is relieved, however, by her down-to-earth attitude and frequent dashes of humour.

The action, sluggish at first, but full of foreboding, develops in insidious fashion. At first the Gülleners and Ill himself think she has come full of goodwill, but numerous hints about death certificates and funerals, not to mention the ornate coffin she brings with her, cause a gradual spread of apprehension, which anticipates and underlines the main action with a kind of contrapuntal effect. The act reaches its climax when she gives her conditions for helping the town: she offers an astronomical sum of money to the townspeople 'wenn jemand Alfred Ill tötet'. The mayor turns down the offer: 'lieber bleiben wir arm denn blutbefleckt!' Her ominous last words, 'Ich warte', are pregnant with meaning, as is often the case at the end of an act in Dürrenmatt.

The setting for the second act is the street containing the hotel, flanked by Ill's shop and the police-station. By her conversations on the balcony, Claire reveals her complete indifference to the drama being enacted below. We are not at first aware that the Gülleners are having second thoughts, but their changed mode of buying shows they have almost unlimited credit, symbolized vividly in their new, yellow shoes. The words 'neue, gelbe Schuhe', 'gelbe, neue Schuhe', make clear the thoughts running through Ill's tortured mind: his betrayal is imminent.

His desperate position, that of the hunted man, is anticipated and drawn into sharp relief by the escape of the black panther which Claire has brought with her, a motif almost certainly taken from real life. Most of the citizens, even the parson, carry rifles, shots are heard, and a high state of tension prevails. The secondary action symbolizes the main action and mingles with it. This use of a significant symbol is a characteristic of the German 'Novelle', but its effective use in the drama is rarer. Stage directions, always meaningful in Dürrenmatt, become eerie: 'Überall an den Wänden werden Güllener sichtbar ... herumspähend, die Gewehre schußbereit, herumschleichend.' Ill's last lingering doubts leave him when he hears the tolling of the parson's new bell. The scene ends with the shooting of the panther before Ill's shop. Resolved to escape, he reaches the station, where he is surrounded by Gülleners, ostensibly wishing him a safe journey, but with every word of well-wishing they increasingly take on the guise of hungry vultures, hovering round their victim. His final, significant words as the act closes, 'Ich bin verloren', mark resignation to his fate.

In a postscript to the play, Dürrenmatt emphasizes the fact that in the station scene the townsfolk have no evil intentions: they accept credit without thinking of the consequences and at the station act only in a friendly manner. Ill is certain of his fate, but their guilt is stealing slowly and surreptitiously upon them: the turning-point for the Gülleners comes only at the beginning of the last act, when the doctor and the teacher visit Claire in the 'Petersche Scheune', another haunt of her youth, and vainly try to make her relent. To their plea for humanity she replies:

'Die Menschlichkeit, meine Herren, ist für die Börse der Millionäre geschaffen . . . anständig ist nur, wer zahlt, und ich zahle. Güllen für einen Mord, Konjunktur für eine Leiche.'

As outward signs of prosperity mount up and opinion turns almost imperceptibly against Ill, the general feeling is crystallized in the words of the drunken teacher: 'Man wird Sie töten, ich weiß es von Anfang an. Die Versuchung ist zu groß und unsere Armut zu bitter.' Ill, by finally accepting his fate, increases in stature; his readiness to sacrifice himself makes him a kinsman of Romulus and not far removed from a Schiller hero.

Claire, too, acts with resignation, indicating that the workings of justice are greater than all human striving, her own included:

'Meine Liebe konnte nicht sterben. Aber auch nicht leben. Sie ist etwas Böses geworden, wie ich selber, wie die bleichen Pilze und die blinden Wurzelgesichter in diesem Wald, überwuchert von meinen goldenen Milliarden. Die haben nach dir gegriffen mit ihren Fangarmen, dein Leben zu suchen.'

This speech in the Konradsweilerwald reflects some of the darker, uncanny aspects of the German fairy-tale, a direct contrast with the mood of hilarity prevailing in *Ein Engel*.

The final scene, in the 'Theatersaal' of the hotel, attended by all the glare of modern publicity — Press, radio, television — is ostensibly to accept the bequest, but only the initiated know the terrible condition attached, so that every sentence uttered by the mayor and the teacher has a *double entendre* — one meaning for the world outside and another for the Gülleners. This brings into sharp relief the contrast between the life-and-death drama being enacted and the gay picture of prosperity through charity which is being presented to the world. With the hall in darkness, the moon filtering through the gallery windows on to the shadowy, silent figures, the victim, morally towering over his assailants, is dispatched. To the parson's 'Sie fürchten sich nicht mehr?', he answers 'Nicht mehr sehr', and to the offer 'Ich werde für Sie beten', he pronounces his judgement on the town with the answer 'Beten Sie für Güllen'.

In the postscript Dürrenmatt states that his intention is to portray actual people. Claire is what he says she is: a fabulously rich woman who has been wronged, and not a symbol of the Marshall Plan, modern materialism, or even the apocalypse. The Gülleners are ordinary people and he himself might not have acted differently. While one might agree as regards the Gülleners, Claire is no ordinary person, not even an ordinary millionairess, and is far beyond the limits of natural or psychological probability. Human, warm-blooded personalities, with whom one could identify oneself, are almost entirely lacking in Dürrenmatt's works. Indeed, if Claire displayed any human qualities she would become a monster and the play would be ruined. But she has no feelings at all, only the memories of feelings, no hatred, only a plan worked out years ago.

She has humour, however, a rather brusque humour, and her speech, abrupt, contemptuous, and commanding, further accentuates the gulf between her and the lesser mortals she manipulates: first, her puppet-like following and faceless husbands, who can be played by the same actor; later the citizens of Güllen. The fascination of a figure like Claire lies in the different facets of her personality: the avenging Greek goddess is repeatedly referred to, but when she is on the balcony, awaiting confidently the inevitable issue of the drama of crime and punishment being played out below, the connection with the medieval morality play becomes apparent. At other times, when we see her accompanied by the blind eunuchs or the ex-gangsters — who have first cousins in *Der Prozeß* — the comparison with Kafka is not far to seek.

If Claire is static and aloof, Ill's character develops from a 'verschmierter Krämer', who imagines that time and life have extirpated all guilt, into a figure of great nobility, who through fear and horror finally comes to recognize his crime and to accept his fate. Towards the end, during the motor-car ride, he becomes an almost poetic figure, revealing a broader, more open outlook, with some of the 'Entrücktheit' that Claire shows throughout the play: 'Wolkenungetüme am Himmel, übereinandergetürmt wie im Sommer. Seh' es heute wie zum ersten Mal!'

Dürrenmatt's main problem in writing the tragi-comedy was to render more acceptable the gruesomeness of the basic theme. The main device used is to give the heroine an aura of remoteness, so that she is more an instrument of justice than an incarnation of wickedness. She is made to exude this other-worldliness, as, for example, when the teacher comments, shortly after seeing her, that he has been marking Greek and Latin exercises for years, but 'Was gruseln heißt, weiß ich erst seit einer Stunde'. Her aloofness is accentuated by the 'depersonalizing' of her entourage, whilst her sense of humour helps to make her more acceptable. Similarly, the harshness of the play as a whole is softened by the introduction of comedy when it is most needed: one thinks particularly of the drunken teacher and the presence of Press, radio, and television in the final scene; tragedy becomes once again 'a terrible moment, an abyss that opens' in the midst of comedy.

All kinds of morals may be read into the play: the corruption of a community — one thinks of Gotthelf's *Die Schwarze Spinne* and Bergengruen's *Der Großtyrann und das Gericht* — through greed, temptation, or fear; the insidious attack of materialism on all our values; even the idea that justice always triumphs in the end, or that life — when one contemplates the inane picture of Claire's entourage or the greed, lying, and hypocrisy of the Gülleners — is 'a tale full of sound and fury, signifying nothing'. Never in any previous work had Dürrenmatt made such a skilful use of the stage and never before had he achieved such a balanced blending of comedy, satire, and drama. In his next work, *Die Physiker*, he moved towards the completely classical concept, but paid the penalty for this with a certain flatness and uniformity, in spite of blood-curdling highlights and comic scenes full of crisp repartee.

Die Physiker

Die Physiker, first staged in Zürich in 1962, has since achieved international acclaim, including a run at the

Aldwych Theatre, London, and in the provinces. In many ways new ground was being broken, the paradox being, however, that this took the form of a reversion to the basic features of the classical Greek drama. In *Theaterprobleme* Dürrenmatt had shown how the unities of time, place, and action had grown out of the cultural and religious background of the ancient Greek theatre, an organic growth that could not flourish under other conditions, except perhaps in the one-act play. Nevertheless, he reserved for himself the right to experiment. One view of *Die Physiker*, with its compact, streamlined form and rigid adherence to the unities, is that it is the culmination and final crystallization of the long series of experiments which begin with *Es steht geschrieben* or even earlier.

The critic of *Die Zeit* considers the play unequalled in German post-war drama, with some reservations in favour of *Der Besuch* and Brecht's productions. It is interesting to compare the play with Brecht's *Das Leben des Galilei* (some critics have called *Die Physiker* a part of Dürrenmatt's 'dialogue' with Brecht), as both plays deal with the basic theme of a scientist at variance with the thought of his times, but whereas in Brecht there is much social criticism, aimed at established authority, Dürrenmatt's concern is to point out the dangers to which science can bring us, especially when so many happenings have a completely irrational basis.[1]

Apart from the control and classical polish of *Die Physiker*, the main impact of the play lies in the fact that the author has succeeded in combining a theatrically very effective comedy with a serious discussion of the scientists'

---

[1] Cf. 'The Scientist in Society' (Brecht, Dürrenmatt, Kipphardt) an article by R. Knight in the Spring 1966 issue of *Germania*. (University of Bristol German Society.)

responsibilities to mankind. Only a dramatist of Dürrenmatt's range of fantasy and great inventive genius could have made a success out of such uncompromising material, and his bold decision to adhere rigidly to classical standards is not only in keeping with the dialectical aspects of the work, but enables these to be given their proper emphasis, without which the comedy might have degenerated into the trivial or the sensational. This is another example of Dürrenmatt's extreme sensitivity and impeccable taste in matters concerning the theatre and is paralleled by his unerring delineation of the heroine in *Der Besuch*.

The main criticisms levelled at the play are twofold: that the more meaningful scenes are flat, dialectical, and lacking in dramatic content; secondly, that little effort is made at characterization. While the latter deficiency applies to most of Dürrenmatt's works — it is due in part to his predilection for comedy — the accusation that there are too many *longueurs* must be considered in the light of the intrinsic difficulty of the theme, with its high intellectual content, which demanded a stricter control of time, place, and action than was necessary in earlier productions. In spite of these restrictions, the play moves along at a brisk pace, mainly owing to originality of plot and cleverness of dialogue, but also because of the burning problems being debated and the speculation as to the outcome.

The unity of action demands a central, unified plot, uncomplicated by any subsidiary happenings; this has to take place in a limited locality, usually a single room, within a period of not more than a single day: these constitute the unities of place and time. A difficulty in observing them is the necessity for a longish 'Vorgeschichte' to make up for the control of time and place. This problem is skilfully solved by making the action revolve mainly round the situation; what little exposition there is fits in perfectly naturally and adds to the comic effect.

The action unfolds itself in the drawing-room of a madhouse *de luxe*, run by an eccentric hunchbacked spinster, Fräulein Doktor Mathilde von Zahnd, one of the class of 'degenerierter Adel'. Her prize patients, living apart from the rest, are three supposedly lunatic physicists: Ernst Heinrich Ernesti, a *soi-disant* Einstein; Herbert Georg Beutler, who imagines he is Sir Isaac Newton; and Wilhelm Möbius, the 'mutiger Mensch' of this play, who has the delusion that he sees visions of King Solomon. This most original choice of setting and characters is a firm basis for comedy, thrills, and a reasoned discussion of the scientist's duty towards his fellows, all three ingredients being so cleverly blended with so many surprising twists and turns that one leaves the theatre in a light-hearted mood, albeit not unmindful of the grim message presented. The general atmosphere created is indeed nearer to the carefree hilarity of *Ein Engel*, without the fairy-tale element, than to the harshness and trenchant severity of *Der Besuch* or *Mississippi*.

Another feature of the play is its almost mathematical precision, which, together with the concise, almost laconic style and the well-marshalled comings and goings of the characters, bears some resemblance to Lessing's *Emilia Galotti*. The physicists each murder their favourite nurse, one before the play starts, one just as the curtain rises, and the last at the close of the first act. The reason, with slight variations, is the same: the nurses have found out that the scientists are far from mad and so threaten to interfere with their plans.

The 'Hitchcock' atmosphere is discreetly suffused and alternated with scenes and dialogues of comic relief, especially in the first act, so that the murders have an air of unreality or unimportance, not unlike the hangings and threatened hangings of *Ein Engel*: we are not far removed from the world of the 'Wiener Volkstheater'. It may be felt that in creating this flippant atmosphere Dürrenmatt was letting himself go just a little too far and thereby vitiating the general impression of the play, more particularly its serious impact and the human appeal of the characters. The superficial answer to this is that 'Ulk' and 'Jux' are an integral part of Dürrenmatt's make-up, of more importance to him than characterization. Few of his figures are as firmly based in nature or psychology as those of Frisch. Between comedy and dialectical argument, they seem to forfeit all individuality: the wit, satire, and repartee, shared by so many, rob each one of individuality, even though we have the excuse that they are supposed to be lunatics. There is, however, a deeper answer, to which we shall revert later: that the characters were intended to be portrayed as puppets, a prey to grim reality or base chance, mechanical themselves in an action which moves with mathematical precision towards the inevitable end — the destruction of their hopes and plans.

One function of the subsidiary characters, apart from filling in the picture, is to supply this comic relief and prepare us for the coming of the main characters. We first meet the rather whimsical, dry-humoured Inspector Voß, perhaps the best-drawn character, who is crossing swords with Oberschwester Marta Boll, 'die so resolut aussieht, wie sie heißt und ist'. She is not at all certain that the murder wouldn't have happened with male nurses, as

INTRODUCTION

Dorothea Moser was a member of the Ladies' Wrestling Club, and Irene Straub, the other victim, a judo champion. Asked by the ever-patient Inspector what her line is, she answers: 'Ich stemme' ('I'm a weight-lifter'). This use of exaggeration, the paradoxical, or the incongruous in all its forms to achieve comical, satirical, or theatrical effects is an ever-dominant feature of Dürrenmatt's works. It is next in evidence when the Inspector wishes to see the murderer Einstein, but isn't allowed to because '[er]muß jetzt geigen', or when Newton, himself a murderer, says: 'Wie kann ein Mensch nur eine Krankenschwester erdrosseln!' Eventually Einstein drops off to sleep, soothed by his fiddling, and his accompanist, the Fräulein Doktor, is at last free to meet the Inspector. She expresses the opinion that exposure to radioactive infection may be the cause of the physicists' eccentricities, but must agree to employ only male nurses in this part of the institution, a decision which motivates the third murder at the end of the act.

Further comedy and exposition are afforded by the arrival of Frau Möbius, accompanied by her new husband, the philoprogenitive missionary Rose, and her three sons. She has come to say good-bye before going abroad on missionary work, and so gives the background of the third and most brilliant scientist, Wilhelm Möbius, who puts on a special act of madness to enable them to leave him with a good conscience. Dürrenmatt frequently livens up his plays by the introduction of characters, oddities in one way or another, who form a complete contrast to the general course of the action or give some light relief. The whole situation here is incongruous: the marriage with Oskar Rose, 'ein leidenschaftlicher Vater' who is 'durchaus nicht robust'; the nine children, three of whom, Möbius's sons, play on their flutes a piece by Buxtehude as a farewell gesture; the paradox in Rose's marriage to another man's wife and his missionary zeal, not to mention Möbius's offhand reaction to the visit, and the 'Psalm of Solomon to be sung to space-travellers' with which he regales his visitors. This grotesque interlude can be matched with the sudden appearance of the white-clad, bespectacled doctors and the Church dignitaries in *Mississippi*, as indeed the paradox of the marriage is paralleled in the veneration offered to Anastasia, the essence of immorality, by the heads of the three Churches. This love of clashing contrasts, of the paradoxical in its most extreme form ranging from the odd remark to a whole situation, or even, as in *Die Physiker* or *Romulus*, to the very structure of the play, is a basic feature of all Dürrenmatt's work. He cannot resist the urge to take hold of accepted conceptions and beliefs and turn them upside-down or inside-out, thereby shocking his audience into serious reflection.

Möbius's antics do not deceive his favourite nurse, Schwester Monika, who has found out his secret: that he has discovered the 'system of all possible inventions'. Male nurses are now taking over, so she pleads with him to flee with her and offer his invention to mankind. As his only reason for coming into the institution was to withhold from the world the terrible consequences of his invention, he has now, in spite of their love, no alternative but to strangle her if he is to keep his secret intact. With minor changes, the murder follows the pattern of the previous two, thus giving the plot the necessary mathematical precision and the author an opportunity to indulge in repetitive dialogues and paradoxical remarks, as the opening of

INTRODUCTION

Act Two is a near-repeat of the beginning of Act One.

At the end of this first act the appetite of the audience has been whetted: three murders have caused a considerable rise in tension; our curiosity as to how the dénouement will work out is similar to that we enjoy while reading a detective story, a branch of writing in which Dürrenmatt excels and which has left its mark on this comedy. We have fairly complete details concerning Möbius, but are wondering how the other two scientists fit in.

There has been little attempt at characterization and most of the minor characters have been cast with a view to comedy, satire, or the grotesque: Marta Boll, the resolute battle-axe, who tries to make all observe the non-smoking, non-drinking rule; the philosophic, laconic, and far from typical Inspector, going through his duties with an air of remoteness, resignation, and mild surprise, who doesn't mind taking the pseudo-madmen on at their own game, as when he tells Newton that he must be over two hundred years old; Frau Möbius and Oskar Rose, rather colourless, but nevertheless adding comical and grotesque touches. The scientists, insisting on their own sanity in the midst of all the outrages, are a cause of constant laughter: Einstein, 'fiddling through' the Kreutzersonate to soothe his nerves after the murder; Newton, complete with wig and seventeenth-century costume, expressing mild surprise on hearing the death-rattle and promptly tidying up the room 'aus Ordnungsliebe'. This all makes for good theatre, the emphasis being on the witty or ironic remark, the incongruous character or situation, and the excitement of the spectator's curiosity rather than on didacticism or delineation of character.

Towards the end of the second and last act the serious

element of the play is revealed — a discussion between the three physicists on the rights and responsibilities of genius. Dürrenmatt's problem was to introduce this dialectical incursion into the action in as natural a manner as possible without forfeiting tension or humour. To a large extent he has succeeded, in spite of the almost complete incompatibility of drama and argumentation. This is due to the variety he brings into the action, and his unerring sense of the theatre, which keeps any tendency towards excessive didacticism in tight check. The method adopted is advocated in *Theaterprobleme*: the public must be 'captured' through inventiveness, originality, wit, and satire. Interest is maintained during the longish, discursive passages because the spoken word takes over and the force of the argument — with interpolated pauses — assumes a dramatic quality.

The corpse may be different, but the dialogue at the beginning of the second act is closely modelled on that of the first. Repetitions of scenes, dialogues, or phrases, usually with slight alterations, sometimes with double meanings, are fairly common in Dürrenmatt and can have different effects: to give extra emphasis; to 'alienate' the audience by making them more conscious of the author than of the actors, thus reducing the stature of the players and giving them a puppet-like quality; finally, to achieve a comic effect by introducing minor changes into the dialogue. Usually there is a combination of these effects. The Inspector's reaction to the third killing is highly amusing and may be summed up in the words 'familiarity breeds contempt'. This time he takes on the mantle of the matron and reprimands Fräulein von Zahnd for using the word 'murder'; he doesn't want to interview Möbius:

'Den überlasse ich Ihnen. ... Mit den andern radioaktiven Physikern.' He is even beginning to enjoy himself: 'Ich genieße es auf einmal. Ich könnte jubeln. Ich habe drei Mörder gefunden, die ich mit gutem Gewissen nicht zu verhaften brauche.' Here is yet another highly paradoxical situation.

Any tendency towards flatness is counteracted by the threatened duel between Einstein and Newton — which, however, has little air of reality — and the grotesque figures who take over as male nurses, all ex-boxing champions, symbols of brute force and violence. They complete the picture of a world which is a prey to suppression and fear, an innuendo of which is given in the stage directions to the first act: 'so daß überall schweigsame und schattenhafte Gruppen und Grüppchen von hackenden und umgrabenden Verbrechern sichtbar sind.'[1] The Negro McArthur and the South American champion Murillo serve 'für die lieben Kranken' a sumptuous meal — 'Die reinste Henkersmahlzeit' — always the occasion in Dürrenmatt's works for important developments. Other examples of this are in *Die Panne*, one of the best of the prose writings, and *Der Richter und sein Henker*, in both of which the fate of the culprit is sealed during a hearty meal. Akki's success in outmanœuvring the otherwise incorruptible hangman is achieved in a similar manner. Dürrenmatt's love of the paradoxical, of glaring contrasts, causes him to make full use of this motif: the pleasure of a good meal is a prelude to the complete discomfiture, even

---

[1] The intentional pairing of words in this passage is an interesting feature of Dürrenmatt's style and is found in Goethe, Hesse and others. *Dichtung und Wahrheit* and *Das Glasperlenspiel* offer good examples.

the death, of one of the participants, and often the momentary enjoyment leads to a confession which has lasting and very unpleasant consequences.

Conversations between the scientists during and after the meal reveal the facts of the case: all are perfectly sane; Newton and Einstein are working for opposing Great Powers — the reference to America and Russia is obvious — in an effort to kidnap Möbius, whose inventions would give them control over the world, but would, in Möbius's view, lead to mass destruction. In a reasoned argument between the three, Möbius's opinion prevails: he has the responsibility for his discovery and rather than expose it to misuse he will deny it to mankind. He has little difficulty in refuting their objections:

'Jeder preist mir eine andere Theorie an, doch die Realität, die man mir bietet, ist dieselbe: Ein Gefängnis. Da ziehe ich mein Irrenhaus vor. Es gibt mir wenigstens die Sicherheit, von Politikern nicht ausgenützt zu werden.'

He does not intend to assist in exposing mankind to the possibility of total annihilation. When Einstein objects that they'll have to stay in the sanatorium for life because 'Gescheiterten Spionen kräht kein Hahn mehr nach', Möbius is unmoved:

'Meine einzige Chance, doch noch unentdeckt zu bleiben. Nur im Irrenhaus sind wir noch frei. Nur im Irrenhaus dürfen wir noch denken. In der Freiheit sind unsere Gedanken Sprengstoff.'[1]

His murder was to avoid a mass murder throughout

[1] Note how the sentences are of nearly equal length, based on a seven-word unit. This balancing of short sentences against each other is used consistently throughout the play and is in keeping with the laconic style and classical structure.

the world, as he tells them in the following passage:

'Sollen unsere Morde sinnlos werden? Entweder haben wir geopfert oder gemordet. Entweder bleiben wir im Irrenhaus oder die Welt wird eines. Entweder löschen wir uns im Gedächtnis der Menschen aus oder die Menschheit erlischt.'

To this the only answer is silence, usually in Dürrenmatt the prelude to an important decision: Möbius's arguments are accepted by Einstein and Newton — their real names are Eisler and Kilton — who agree to stay. The course of the argument has been a little flat, as the telling points made by Möbius seem to make the outcome a foregone conclusion.

It can be fairly safely assumed that Möbius's doctrine of the responsibility of the individual is a reflection of Dürrenmatt's own views. Satirical thrusts at those who push off the blame on to others issuing orders occur frequently in his works. One can contrast Akki's defiance of all authority, rounded off by the advice 'so muß man schäbige Berufe ausüben', with the almost identical excuses Einstein and Newton make for their murders: 'Der Vorfall tut mir außerordentlich leid.... Befehl ist Befehl.... Ich konnte nicht anders handeln.... Meine Mission stand in Frage....' This repeated dialogue, reducing the two scientists to the status of marionettes, fits in well with the mathematical pattern on which the play is built. A similar repetition, rather like a parody of the Greek chorus, occurs after the three have made their decision. They offer a solemn toast to each of the dead nurses and finally retire to their rooms in an exalted mood, satisfied with the sacrifice they are making.

As must be expected in Dürrenmatt, the inevitable sharp contrast, the pricking of the balloon of pious self-satisfaction, is not long delayed, and the final twist to the action, announced by the appearance of the Fräulein Doktor and her gangster-like guards, is symbolized by the replacement of Geheimrat August von Zahnd's portrait by that of General Leonidas von Zahnd: the step from peace to war has been made. The former appellation 'die lieben Kranken' now becomes 'Rauskommen!', and the scientists, in sentences which are structurally very similar, sing the praises of the night in a last vain effort to retain the façade of madness: 'Eine andächtige Nacht. Tiefblau und fromm . . .', 'Eine geheimnisvolle Nacht. Unendlich und erhaben . . .', 'Eine glückliche Nacht. Tröstlich und gut. . . .' Besides conforming with the repetitive dialogue this semi-poetical language is purposely brought in to form as sharp a contrast as possible to the unpleasant incidents which follow. Ill is in a similar exalted mood and uses comparable language, already quoted, prior to his last fateful meeting with the Gülleners (see above, p. liii).

In a scene which could be taken from a detective novel, the scientists are told that their game is up, disarmed, and robbed of their secret transmitters. Iron bars which have been dropped down outside the windows already give the room a prison-like appearance; this is intensified when the prisoners are confronted with the glare of searchlights. Once again the setting is changed to accord with the reduced status of the characters; the stage is being used as an instrument, to corroborate and supplement the spoken word. As in *Der Besuch*, the atmosphere chosen for the climax is theatrically very effective and in keeping with the grim news purveyed to the victims, the greatest paradox of many to be found in the play. Fräulein von Zahnd now asserts that she has visions of Solomon, has been entrusted with all his secrets, and has photostat copies of all Möbius's manuscripts, by means of which she can exploit the whole world. There is much comedy in the paradoxical situation of the three erstwhile lunatics frantically telling the Doctor she is mad, culminating in Newton's desperate assertion: 'Sie sind übergeschnappt! Vollkommen! Begreifen Sie doch endlich! (*leise*) Wir sind alle übergeschnappt.'

The scene abounds in irony and paradox: firstly, that the Fräulein Doktor should suddenly become the person we suspect to be mad; secondly, that all the guile, forethought, and intelligence of the three scientists have only served to bring about a far more disastrous issue than the one they had been avoiding; thirdly, that their murders, unwillingly committed to keep their secrets intact, had been planned and foreseen by the eccentric spinster so that she would have no trouble in restricting their freedom, thus enabling her to achieve world dominion.

Einstein's words, 'Die Welt ist in die Hände einer verrückten Irrenärztin gefallen', sum up the despair and resignation of the physicists, who have made a courageous, high-minded, and sacrificial effort to enable 'Geist' to conquer 'die Materie Mensch', but like Romulus and others they have been routed by reality or, as it is called in the postscript, 'der Zufall'. The only answer is to carry on with the comedy of human absurdity, if they are allowed to.

The comedy concludes with short statements to the audience by the three physicists. Each tells who he is supposed to be and what he has done with his life. Their observations follow the same pattern and show Dürrenmatt's meticulous attention to points of style. Newton and Einstein each repeat three sentences from the beginning of their statements before retiring to their rooms. Möbius begins with: 'Ich bin Salomo. Ich bin der arme König Salomo.' As the next sentence was apparently too long to bear repetition at the end and might have destroyed the balance of the concluding words, Dürrenmatt simply repeats the first sentence, so the play ends with: 'Ich bin Salomo, ich bin Salomo, ich bin der arme König Salomo.' The resemblance to the chorus of the ancient Greek drama is obvious.

These short, final statements are not without significance. Einstein expresses succinctly one of life's major paradoxes: 'Ich liebe die Menschen und liebe meine Geige, aber auf meine Empfehlung hin baute man die Atombombe.' A related idea is expressed in the postscript to *Ein Engel*: 'Alle sind gegen den Turm und dennoch kommt er zustande. . . .' This was to have been the gist of a further play about Babylon. Dürrenmatt is here giving expression to one of his basic beliefs: that each and every individual does bear the responsibility for his actions, and that only if all accept this responsibility can there be any hope of solving mankind's problems.[1] The alternative is the doom foretold by Möbius in his final speech: 'irgendwo, um einen kleinen, gelben, namenlosen Stern, kreist, sinnlos, immerzu, die radioaktive Erde.' A similar fate was prophesied to the self-seeking Gülleners in the stage directions for the last chorus: 'zwei Chöre bildend, . . . als

---

[1] There is, in Dürrenmatt, some suggestion of a connection between this doctrine of personal responsibility and the Christian conception of Grace; cf. especially Knipperdollinck's dying speech in *Es steht geschrieben* and Ill's acceptance of his fate.

gäbe ein havariertes Schiff, weit abgetrieben, die letzten Signale!'[1]

The style of *Die Physiker* stems from the strictly classical concept of the play and the almost mathematical precision evident not only in the dramatic structure, but in individual speeches and dialogues. One essential feature of a classical play is control, which starts with the unities and reaches its fulfilment in the polish and accuracy of the language. Dürrenmatt is most precise in the rhythmical balance of his clauses and sentences, which throughout the whole play are kept as short as possible and usually of equal length. An extension of this is the crispness of the dialogue — short, sharp questions and answers, frequently monosyllabic or consisting of one or two words, often of similar length, not unlike the stichomythia of classical Greek drama. A further feature, already mentioned, is the repetition of dialogues or the use of alternating speeches of similar length and content, such as the toasts of the scientists or their concluding addresses. Apart from giving the comedy a classical polish, this is probably intended to give a puppet-like mechanical quality to the main characters, to whom at one stage the Fräulein Doktor says: 'Mit eurem Handeln konnte ich rechnen. Ihr waret bestimmbar wie Automaten und habt getötet wie Henker.' They had hoped to improve the world by their independent actions, but like other courageous men in Dürrenmatt's works they have no more control over the ultimate outcome of their actions than have marionettes, geniuses though they all are.

The twenty-one explanatory points forming the post-

[1] '... forming two choirs, ... as if a damaged ship, drifting far off course, were sending out its last signals.'

script to the play are an elucidation of the writer's approach to his task and an indication of the possible effect on the spectator. The basic idea, summarized in the last point, is that the playwright should try by every means in his power to bring his audience face to face with reality, in this case the grim spectre of nuclear war and the possible extinction of our planet. The same idea, with the implied serious view of the artist's mission, was expressed at the end of *Theaterprobleme*.[1] The prevention of this major disaster is the concern of all, and any individual efforts towards a solution are doomed to failure. Such is the message of the play, rather than any attempt to place the burden squarely on the shoulders of the scientist. It does not mean, however, that the genius has no responsibility for the fruits of his invention; the whole tenor of the comedy stresses the great burden of the scientist, but indicates that withholding of knowledge for reasons of conscience can only be, at the best, temporarily successful, like Romulus's and Odoaker's efforts to govern on rational lines. This point is made by Fräulein Doktor von Zahnd at the end of the last act: she says of Möbius's discovery: 'Denn was ihm offenbart worden war, ist kein Geheimnis. Weil es denkbar ist. Alles Denkbare wird einmal gedacht. Jetzt oder in der Zukunft.' It is useless to burke the issue by hiding away.

[1] It is interesting to compare Schiller's view of the function of art, as expressed in *Über die ästhetische Erziehung des Menschen*: the physical or life urge puts man within the limits of time and makes him 'Materie', a prey to the forces of nature, within and outside him; the artist must seek to develop man first aesthetically, as only by this means is the final aim, a complete moral development, possible. Dürrenmatt, whose phrase 'die Materie Mensch' may originate from Schiller, is pessimistic as to the victory of the spiritual over the material (cf. the ending of *Romulus*).

The general conclusions to be drawn are fairly pessimistic: 'reality' or 'chance' always has the last word and the more men plan to achieve a certain goal, the more likely it is that they will become enmeshed in the workings of an irrational fate.[1] This happens in *Die Physiker* and *Oedipus*, which, in terms of the conflict and the final outcome, show a striking similarity. The Fate of the Greek drama is replaced in Dürrenmatt by chance, but the characters are still brought down to size, even though overweening pride is not specifically mentioned. A feature of many good tragedies is 'Fallhöhe', the fall from greatness: the greater the fall, the greater the tragic effect. This occurs often in Shakespeare, Sophocles, and Hebbel. In Schiller there is a slight change of emphasis, as the tragic is related to the severity of the struggle to maintain moral integrity: the greater the struggle and the sacrifice, the greater the tragic effect. Dürrenmatt, however, could see no firm moral basis for tragedy in our modern society, so he uses the 'Fallhöhe' resulting from excessive scheming and prognosticating, which is greatest and most paradoxical when 'Planmäßigkeit', thwarted by blind chance, rebounds on the heads of the planners and brings about a result opposite to the one desired. This is to be expected, particularly amidst the absurdities and excesses of our modern civilization. Such is the reality which Dürrenmatt as a serious artist has tried to point out to his fellows. The answer is given by the courageous people, typified in Akki, Übelohe, Romulus, and Möbius, who are trying to face up to this monster of a world, but only a concerted effort on the part of all can offer any hope of a solution. This 'defeat' of his heroes affords yet another example of Dürrenmatt's love of paradox.

[1] Cf. also the part played by chance in Hardy's novels.

A striking illustration of the irrational nature of reality is afforded by a comparison of the many attempts on Hitler's life,[1] all doomed to failure in spite of most intelligent planning, with the freak chance that resulted in President Kennedy's death. An apt postscript to *Die Physiker* could be taken from the last letter of a conspirator against Hitler, before his gruesome execution in Berlin: he considered he had been foolish 'als kleiner Mensch Gott hochmütig in den Arm fallen zu wollen'.[2] A fellow conspirator said that he would die with a clear conscience, knowing he had done all he possibly could. Dürrenmatt's heroes are compounded of both these attitudes, but his sympathy lies with the second of the two.

Conclusion

Any attempt to summarize the general features of Dürrenmatt's dramatic works must take into account the statement that his was a drama of experiment. Even so, in the plays discussed, there has been a development towards control and polish, culminating in *Die Physiker*. It would be surprising if future plays followed the classical pattern, however, and this is in part confirmed by the next stage production, a revised version of the radio play *Herkules und der Stall des Augias*.

Certain characteristics stand out in spite of the great variety and originality of his works. Dramatic effect is invariably achieved by exaggeration in many forms, but particularly of character and situation. The grotesque is a

---

[1] See T. Prittie, *Germans against Hitler*, Hutchinson, London, 1964.
[2] '... as a mere mortal to make an arrogant attempt to stay God's arm' (i.e. stop his purpose).

basic ingredient in his plays, reflecting this mad, modern world and urging its citizens to assume responsibility and use God's gifts as they were intended. Most of the leading figures are larger than life and many are caricatures rather than real persons; the recipe for 'capturing' the public is to put such characters together in a *milieu* which has explosive potentialities. The first three plays have a background of war or its aftermath; *Mississippi* is in a setting of revolution and anarchy; *Ein Engel* and *Der Besuch* require a quite extraordinary event to trigger off the action; whilst in *Die Physiker* and *Herkules* a highly original situation is the mainspring of the play. Dürrenmatt's use of exaggerated or outstanding characters or settings makes him a not very distant cousin of Schiller, with, however, a considerable dash of humour, battling unsuccessfully and rather uncertainly against an irrational, grim reality, without the backing of a fixed moral order.

Other vital ingredients of Dürrenmatt's theatre are paradox, parody, contrast, and satire, which are used to debunk power-hungry political or military despots, and to place before the public, in characters such as Akki or Romulus, a sane, rational, and really humane view of how our civilization should be maintained and what values and standards we should esteem. This didactic element results from the dramatist's serious view of the artist's mission and makes him a much more positive playwright than, for instance, Ionesco or Beckett. He is in the tradition of Gotthelf and Keller, his feet planted firmly on the ground, advocating to all, with all the skill and cunning at his disposal, bravery and good humour in the battle against this monster of a world, so that something good may yet come out of the 'Wurstelei unseres Jahrhunderts'.

DIE PHYSIKER
EINE KOMÖDIE IN ZWEI AKTEN

FÜR THERESE GIEHSE

Personen

FRÄULEIN DOKTOR MATHILDE VON ZAHND	*Irrenärztin*
MARTA BOLL	*Oberschwester*
MONIKA STETTLER	*Krankenschwester*
UWE SIEVERS	*Oberpfleger*
MCARTHUR	*Pfleger*
MURILLO	*Pfleger*
HERBERT GEORG BEUTLER, *genannt* NEWTON	*Patient*
ERNST HEINRICH ERNESTI, *genannt* EINSTEIN	*Patient*
JOHANN WILHELM MÖBIUS	*Patient*
MISSIONAR OSKAR ROSE	
FRAU MISSIONAR LINA ROSE	
ADOLF-FRIEDRICH	
WILFRIED-KASPAR	} *Ihre Buben*
JÖRG-LUKAS	
RICHARD VOSS	*Kriminalinspektor*
GERICHTSMEDIZINER	
GUHL	*Polizist*
BLOCHER	*Polizist*

* An asterisk in the text indicates that there is a note at the end of the volume.

ERSTER AKT

Ort: Salon einer bequemen, wenn auch etwas verlotterten ‚Villa'
des privaten Sanatoriums ‚Les Cerisiers'. Nähere Umgebung.
Zuerst natürliches, dann verbautes Seeufer, später eine mittlere,
beinahe kleine Stadt. Das einst schmucke Nest mit seinem Schloß
und seiner Altstadt ist nun mit gräßlichen Gebäuden der Versiche-
rungsgesellschaften verziert und ernährt sich zur Hauptsache von
einer bescheidenen Universität mit ausgebauter theologischer
Fakultät und sommerlichen Sprachkursen, ferner von einer Handels-
und einer Zahntechnikerschule, dann von Töchterpensionaten und
von einer kaum nennenswerten Leichtindustrie und liegt somit schon
an sich abseits vom Getriebe.[1] Dazu beruhigt überflüssigerweise
auch noch die Landschaft die Nerven, jedenfalls sind blaue
Gebirgszüge, human bewaldete[2] Hügel und ein beträchtlicher See
vorhanden, sowie eine weite, abends rauchende Ebene in unmittelbarer Nähe[3] — einst ein düsteres Moor — nun von Kanälen
durchzogen und fruchtbar, mit einer Strafanstalt irgendwo und
dazu gehörendem landwirtschaftlichem Großbetrieb, so daß überall
schweigsame und schattenhafte Gruppen und Grüppchen von
hackenden und umgrabenden Verbrechern sichtbar sind. Doch
spielt das Örtliche eigentlich keine Rolle, wird hier nur der
Genauigkeit zuliebe[4] erwähnt, verlassen wir doch nie die ‚Villa'
des Irrenhauses (nun ist das Wort doch gefallen[5]) noch präziser:

---

[1] *abseits vom Getriebe:* away from the busy world, off the beaten track.
[2] *human bewaldet:* pleasantly wooded, with pleasant woodlands.
[3] *in unmittelbarer Nähe:* in the immediate neighbourhood.
[4] *der Genauigkeit zuliebe:* for the sake of accuracy.
[5] *nun ist das Wort doch gefallen:* now we've let the word slip out after all.

Auch den Salon werden wir nie verlassen, haben wir uns doch vorgenommen, die Einheit von Raum, Zeit und Handlung* streng einzuhalten; einer Handlung, die unter Verrückten spielt, kommt nur die klassische Form bei.[1] *Doch zur Sache. Was die „Villa" betrifft, so waren in ihr einst sämtliche Patienten der Gründerin des Unternehmens Fräulein Dr. h. c.*[2] *Dr. med. Mathilde von Zahnd untergebracht, vertrottelte Aristokraten, arteriosklerotische Politiker — falls sie nicht noch regieren — debile Millionäre, schizophrene Schriftsteller, manisch-depressive Großindustrielle, usw., kurz, die ganze geistig verwirrte Elite des halben Abendlandes, denn das Fräulein Doktor ist berühmt, nicht nur weil die bucklige Jungfer in ihrem ewigen Ärztekittel einer mächtigen autochthonen*[3] *Familie entstammt, deren letzter nennenswerter Sproß sie ist, sondern auch als Menschenfreund und Psychiater von Ruf, man darf ruhig behaupten: Von Weltruf (ihr Briefwechsel mit C. G. Jung* ist eben erschienen). Doch nun sind die prominenten und nicht immer angenehmen Patienten längst in den eleganten, lichten Neubau übergesiedelt, für die horrenden Preise wird auch die bösartigste Vergangenheit ein reines Vergnügen.*[4] *Der Neubau breitet sich im südlichen Teil des weitläufigen Parks in verschiedenen Pavillons aus (mit Ernis Glasmalereien* in der Kapelle) gegen die Ebene zu, während sich von der „Villa" der mit riesigen Bäumen bestückte Rasen zum See hinunterläßt. Dem Ufer entlang führt eine Steinmauer. Im Salon der nun schwach bevölkerten „Villa" halten sich meistens drei Patienten auf, zufälligerweise Physiker, oder doch*

---

[1] *einer Handlung . . . kommt nur die klassische Form bei*: only the classical form is appropriate for, is equal to, an action . . . . (The irony of this remark is obvious.)

[2] *h.c.*: *honoris causa*, honorary (of a degree).

[3] *autochthon*: indigenous, long-established.

[4] *für die horrenden Preise . . . ein reines Vergnügen*: the enormous prices enable even patients with a most wicked past to lead a very pleasant existence.

DIE PHYSIKER

nicht ganz zufälligerweise, man wendet humane Prinzipien an und läßt beisammen, was zusammengehört. Sie leben für sich, jeder eingesponnen in seine eingebildete Welt, nehmen die Mahlzeiten im Salon gemeinsam ein, diskutieren bisweilen über ihre Wissenschaft oder glotzen still vor sich hin, harmlose, liebenswerte Irre, lenkbar, leicht zu behandeln und anspruchslos. Mit einem Wort, sie gäben wahre Musterpatienten ab,[1] wenn nicht in der letzten Zeit Bedenkliches, ja geradezu Gräßliches vorgekommen wäre: Einer von ihnen erdrosselte vor drei Monaten eine Krankenschwester, und nun hat sich der gleiche Vorfall aufs neue ereignet. So ist denn wieder die Polizei im Hause. Der Salon deshalb mehr als üblich bevölkert. Die Krankenschwester liegt auf dem Parkett, in tragischer und definitiver Stellung, mehr im Hintergrund, um das Publikum nicht unnötig zu erschrecken. Doch ist nicht zu übersehen, daß ein Kampf stattgefunden hat. Die Möbel sind beträchtlich durcheinandergeraten. Eine Stehlampe und zwei Sessel liegen auf dem Boden und links vorne ist ein runder Tisch umgekippt, in der Weise, daß nun die Tischbeine dem Zuschauer entgegenstarren. Im übrigen hat der Umbau in ein Irrenhaus (die Villa war einst der von Zahnd'sche Sommersitz) im Salon schmerzliche Spuren hinterlassen. Die Wände sind bis auf Mannshöhe mit hygienischer Lackfarbe überstrichen, dann erst kommt der darunterliegende Gips zum Vorschein,[2] mit zum Teil noch erhaltenen Stukkaturen. Die drei Türen im Hintergrund, die von einer kleinen Halle in die Krankenzimmer der Physiker führen, sind mit schwarzem Leder gepolstert. Außerdem sind sie numeriert eins bis drei. Links neben der Halle ein häßlicher Zentralheizungskörper, rechts ein Lavabo mit Handtüchern an einer Stange. Aus dem Zimmer Nummer zwei (das mittlere Zimmer) dringt Geigenspiel mit

[1] *gäben wahre Musterpatienten ab*: would seem to be really model patients.

[2] *dann ... Vorschein*: only above that can the plaster underneath be seen.

Klavierbegleitung. Beethoven.* Kreutzersonate.* Links befindet sich die Parkfront, die Fenster hoch und bis zum Parkett herunterreichend, der¹ mit Linoleum bedeckt ist. Links und rechts der Fensterfront ein schwerer Vorhang. Die Flügeltüre führt auf eine Terrasse, deren Steingeländer sich vom Park und dem relativ sonnigen Novemberwetter abhebt. Es ist kurz nach halb fünf nachmittags. Rechts über einem nutzlosen Kamin, vor das ein Gitter gestellt ist, hängt das Porträt eines spitzbärtigen alten Mannes in schwerem Goldrahmen. Rechts vorne eine schwere Eichentüre. Von der braunen Kassettendecke* schwebt ein schwerer Kronleuchter. Die Möbel: Beim runden Tisch stehen — ist der Salon aufgeräumt² — drei Stühle: wie der Tisch weiß gestrichen. Die übrigen Möbel leicht zerschlissen, verschiedene Epochen. Rechts vorne ein Sofa mit Tischchen, von zwei Sesseln flankiert. Die Stehlampe gehört eigentlich hinter das Sofa, das Zimmer demnach durchaus nicht überfüllt: Zur Ausstattung einer Bühne, auf der im Gegensatz zu den Stücken der Alten das Satyrspiel* der Tragödie vorangeht, gehört wenig. Wir können beginnen. Um die Leiche bemühen sich Kriminalbeamte, zivil kostümiert, seelenruhige, gemütliche Burschen, die schon ihre Portion Weißwein konsumiert haben und danach riechen. Sie messen, nehmen Fingerabdrücke usw. In der Mitte des Salons steht Kriminalinspektor Richard Voß, in Hut und Mantel, links Oberschwester Marta Boll, die so resolut aussieht, wie sie heißt und ist.³ Auf dem Sessel rechts außen sitzt ein Polizist und stenographiert. Der Kriminalinspektor nimmt eine Zigarre aus einem braunen Etui

---

¹ *Parkett* is usually neuter.
² *ist der Salon aufgeräumt*: if the drawing-room is tidied up.
³ *wie sie heißt und ist*: as she is called and is. (*Das Bollwerk* = bastion or bulwark.)

DIE PHYSIKER

INSPEKTOR. Man darf doch rauchen?
OBERSCHWESTER. Es ist nicht üblich.
INSPEKTOR. Pardon.

(*Er steckt die Zigarre zurück*)

OBERSCHWESTER. Eine Tasse Tee?
INSPEKTOR. Lieber Schnaps.
OBERSCHWESTER. Sie befinden sich in einer Heilanstalt.
INSPEKTOR. Dann nichts. Blocher, du kannst photographieren.
BLOCHER. Jawohl, Herr Inspektor.

(*Man photographiert. Blitzlichter*)

INSPEKTOR. Wie hieß die Schwester?
OBERSCHWESTER. Irene Straub.
INSPECTOR. Alter?
OBERSCHWESTER. Zweiundzwanzig. Aus Kohlwang.
INSPEKTOR. Angehörige?
OBERSCHWESTER. Ein Bruder in der Ostschweiz.
INSPEKTOR. Benachrichtigt?
OBERSCHWESTER. Telephonisch.
INSPEKTOR. Der Mörder? —
OBERSCHWESTER. Bitte, Herr Inspektor — der arme Mensch ist doch krank.
INSPEKTOR. Also gut: Der Täter?
OBERSCHWESTER. Ernst Heinrich Ernesti. Wir nennen ihn Einstein.*
INSPEKTOR. Warum?
OBERSCHWESTER. Weil er sich für Einstein hält.
INSPEKTOR. Ach so.

(*Er wendet sich zum stenographierenden Polizisten*)

Haben Sie die Aussagen der Oberschwester, Guhl?

GUHL. Jawohl, Herr Inspektor.
INSPEKTOR. Erdrosselt, Doktor?
GERICHTSMEDIZINER. Eindeutig. Mit der Schnur der Stehlampe. Diese Irren entwickeln oft gigantische Kräfte. Es hat etwas Großartiges.
INSPEKTOR. So. Finden Sie. Dann finde ich es unverantwortlich, diese Irren von Schwestern pflegen zu lassen. Das ist nun schon der zweite Mord —
OBERSCHWESTER. Bitte, Herr Inspektor.
INSPEKTOR. — der zweite Unglücksfall innert drei Monaten in der Anstalt Les Cerisiers.

(*Er zieht ein Notizbuch hervor*)

Am zwölften August erdrosselte ein Herbert Georg Beutler, der sich für den großen Physiker Newton* hält, die Krankenschwester Dorothea Moser.

(*Er steckt das Notizbuch wieder ein.*)

Auch in diesem Salon. Mit Pflegern wäre das nie vorgekommen.
OBERSCHWESTER. Glauben Sie? Schwester Dorothea Moser war Mitglied des Damenringvereins und Schwester Irene Straub Landesmeisterin des nationalen Judoverbandes.
INSPEKTOR. Und Sie?
OBERSCHWESTER. Ich stemme.
INSPEKTOR. Kann ich nun den Mörder —
OBERSCHWESTER. Bitte, Herr Inspektor.
INSPEKTOR. — den Täter sehen?
OBERSCHWESTER. Er geigt.
INSPEKTOR. Was heißt: Er geigt?
OBERSCHWESTER. Sie hören es ja.

DIE PHYSIKER 7

INSPEKTOR. Dann soll er bitte aufhören.
(*Da die Oberschwester nicht reagiert*)
Ich habe ihn zu vernehmen.
OBERSCHWESTER. Geht nicht.[1]
INSPEKTOR. Warum geht es nicht?
OBERSCHWESTER. Das können wir ärztlich nicht zulassen. Herr Ernesti muß jetzt geigen.
INSPEKTOR. Der Kerl erdrosselte schließlich eine Krankenschwester!
OBERSCHWESTER. Herr Inspektor. Es handelt sich nicht um einen Kerl, sondern um einen kranken Menschen, der sich beruhigen muß. Und weil er sich für Einstein hält, beruhigt er sich nur, wenn er geigt.
INSPEKTOR. Bin ich eigentlich verrückt?
OBERSCHWESTER. Nein.
INSPEKTOR. Man kommt ganz durcheinander.
(*Er wischt sich den Schweiß ab*)
Heiß hier.
OBERSCHWESTER. Durchaus nicht.
INSPEKTOR. Oberschwester Marta. Holen Sie bitte die Chefärztin.
OBERSCHWESTER. Geht auch nicht. Fräulein Doktor begleitet Einstein auf dem Klavier. Einstein beruhigt sich nur, wenn Fräulein Doktor ihn begleitet.
INSPEKTOR. Und vor drei Monaten mußte Fräulein Doktor mit Newton Schach spielen, damit sich der beruhigen konnte. Darauf gehe ich nicht mehr ein,[2] Oberschwester Marta. Ich muß die Chefärztin einfach sprechen.

[1] *Geht nicht*: it is impossible.
[2] *Darauf gehe ich nicht mehr ein*: I can't agree to that any more.

OBERSCHWESTER. Bitte. Dann warten Sie eben.
INSPEKTOR. Wie lange dauert das Gegeige noch?
OBERSCHWESTER. Eine Viertelstunde, eine Stunde. Je nach dem.¹

(*Der Inspektor beherrscht sich*)

INSPEKTOR. Schön. Ich warte.

(*Er brüllt*)

Ich warte!
BLOCHER. Wir wären fertig, Herr Inspektor.
INSPEKTOR (*dumpf*). Und mich macht man fertig.

(*Stille. Der Inspektor wischt sich den Schweiß ab*)

Ihr könnt die Leiche hinausschaffen.
BLOCHER. Jawohl, Herr Inspektor.
OBERSCHWESTER. Ich zeige den Herren den Weg durch den Park in die Kapelle.

(*Sie öffnet die Flügeltüre. Die Leiche wird hinausgetragen. Ebenso die Instrumente. Der Inspektor nimmt den Hut ab, setzt sich erschöpft auf den Sessel links vom Sofa. Immer noch Geigenspiel, Klavierbegleitung. Da kommt aus Zimmer Nummer 3 Herbert Georg Beutler in einem Kostüm des beginnenden achtzehnten Jahrhunderts mit Perücke*)

NEWTON. Sir Isaak Newton.
INSPEKTOR. Kriminalinspektor Richard Voß.

(*Er bleibt sitzen*)

NEWTON. Erfreut. Sehr erfreut. Wirklich. Ich hörte Gepolter, Stöhnen, Röcheln, dann Menschen kommen und gehen. Darf ich fragen, was sich hier abspielt?

¹ *Je nach dem*: it all depends.

DIE PHYSIKER 9

INSPEKTOR. Schwester Irene Straub wurde erdrosselt.
NEWTON. Die Landesmeisterin des nationalen Judoverbandes?
INSPEKTOR. Die Landesmeisterin.
NEWTON. Schrecklich.
INSPEKTOR. Von Ernst Heinrich Ernesti.
NEWTON. Aber der geigt doch.
INSPEKTOR. Er muß sich beruhigen.
NEWTON. Der Kampf wird ihn auch angestrengt haben. Er ist ja eher schmächtig. Womit hat er —?
INSPEKTOR. Mit der Schnur der Stehlampe.
NEWTON. Mit der Schnur der Stehlampe. Auch eine Möglichkeit. Dieser Ernesti. Er tut mir leid. Außerordentlich. Und auch die Judomeisterin tut mir leid.¹ Sie gestatten. Ich muß etwas aufräumen.
INSPEKTOR. Bitte. Der Tatbestand ist aufgenommen.²

(*Newton stellt den Tisch, dann die Stühle auf*)

NEWTON. Ich ertrage Unordnung nicht. Ich bin eigentlich nur Physiker aus Ordnungsliebe geworden.

(*Er stellt die Stehlampe auf*)

Um die scheinbare Unordnung in der Natur auf eine höhere Ordnung zurückzuführen.³

(*Er zündet sich eine Zigarette an*)

Stört es Sie, wenn ich rauche?

¹ *Er tut mir leid . . . auch die Judomeisterin tut mir leid*: I'm sorry for him . . . also for the women's judo champion.
² *Der Tatbestand ist aufgenommen*: the facts of the case have been taken down.
³ *Um die scheinbare Unordnung . . . zurückzuführen*: in order to show that the seeming disorder in Nature is due to a higher order.

FRIEDRICH DÜRRENMATT

INSPEKTOR (*freudig*). Im Gegenteil, ich —

(*Er will sich eine Zigarre aus seinem Etui nehmen*)

NEWTON. Entschuldigen Sie, doch weil wir gerade von Ordnung gesprochen haben: Hier dürfen nur die Patienten rauchen und nicht die Besucher. Sonst wäre gleich der ganze Salon verpestet.

INSPEKTOR. Verstehe.

(*Er steckt sein Etui wieder ein*)

NEWTON. Stört es Sie, wenn ich ein Gläschen Kognak —?
INSPEKTOR. Durchaus nicht.

(*Newton holt hinter dem Kamingitter eine Kognakflasche und ein Glas hervor*)

NEWTON. Dieser Ernesti. Ich bin ganz durcheinander. Wie kann ein Mensch nur eine Krankenschwester erdrosseln!

(*Er setzt sich aufs Sofa, schenkt sich Kognak ein*)

INSPEKTOR. Dabei haben Sie ja auch eine Krankenschwester erdrosselt.
NEWTON. Ich?
INSPEKTOR. Schwester Dorothea Moser.
NEWTON. Die Ringerin?
INSPEKTOR. Am zwölften August. Mit der Vorhangkordel.
NEWTON. Aber das ist doch etwas ganz anderes, Herr Inspektor. Ich bin schließlich nicht verrückt. Auf Ihr Wohl.[1]
INSPEKTOR. Auf das Ihre.

(*Newton trinkt*)

[1] *Auf Ihr Wohl*: to your health.

NEWTON. Schwester Dorothea Moser. Wenn ich so zurückdenke. Strohblond. Ungemein kräftig. Biegsam trotz ihrer Körperfülle. Sie liebte mich und ich liebte sie. Das Dilemma war nur durch eine Vorhangkordel zu lösen.[1]
INSPEKTOR. Dilemma?
NEWTON. Meine Aufgabe besteht darin, über die Gravitation nachzudenken, nicht ein Weib zu lieben.
INSPEKTOR. Begreife.
NEWTON. Dazu kam noch der enorme Altersunterschied.
INSPEKTOR. Sicher. Sie müssen ja weit über zweihundert Jahre alt sein.

(*Newton starrt ihn verwundert an*)

NEWTON. Wieso?
INSPEKTOR. Nun, als Newton —
NEWTON. Sind Sie nun vertrottelt,[2] Herr Inspektor, oder tun Sie nur so?
INSPEKTOR. Hören Sie —
NEWTON. Sie glauben wirklich, ich sei Newton?
INSPEKTOR. Sie glauben es ja.

(*Newton schaut sich mißtrauisch um*)

NEWTON. Darf ich Ihnen ein Geheimnis anvertrauen, Herr Inskpetor?
INSPEKTOR. Selbstverständlich.

---

[1] *war . . . zu lösen*: could be solved. (After a tense of the verb *sein*, *zu* + an infinitive has the meaning of 'to be' + past participle. Cf. *Was ist zu tun?*: What is to be done? *Das läßt sich nicht machen* That can't be done.)

[2] *vertrottelt*: stupid, dull-witted. (*Der Trottel*, a word of Austrian origin, is applied to a person having hereditary or acquired feeble-mindedness; in many districts it has the same meaning as 'cretin'.)

NEWTON. Ich bin nicht Sir Isaak. Ich gebe mich nur als Newton aus.¹

INSPEKTOR. Und weshalb?

NEWTON. Um Ernesti nicht zu verwirren.

INSPEKTOR. Kapiere ich nicht.²

NEWTON. Im Gegensatz zu mir ist doch Ernesti wirklich krank. Er bildet sich ein, Albert Einstein zu sein.

INSPEKTOR. Was hat das mit Ihnen zu tun?

NEWTON. Wenn Ernesti nun erführe, daß ich in Wirklichkeit Albert Einstein bin, wäre der Teufel los.³

INSPEKTOR. Sie wollen damit sagen —

NEWTON. Jawohl. Der berühmte Physiker und Begründer der Relativitätstheorie bin ich. Geboren am 14. März 1879 in Ulm.

(Der Inspektor erhebt sich etwas verwirrt)

INSPEKTOR. Sehr erfreut.

(Newton erhebt sich ebenfalls)

NEWTON. Nennen Sie mich einfach Albert.

INSPEKTOR. Und Sie mich Richard.

(Sie schütteln sich die Hände)

NEWTON. Ich darf Ihnen versichern, daß ich die Kreutzersonate bei weitem schwungvoller hinunterfiedeln würde als Ernst Heinrich Ernesti eben. Das Andante spielt er doch einfach barbarisch.

INSPEKTOR. Ich verstehe nichts von Musik.

NEWTON. Setzen wir uns.

¹ *Ich gebe mich nur als Newton aus*: I only pretend I am Newton.
² *Kapiere ich nicht*: I can't follow you, can't understand.
³ *wäre der Teufel los*: hell would be let loose.

(*Er zieht ihn aufs Sofa. Newton legt den Arm um die Schulter des Inspektors*)

Richard.
INSPEKTOR. Albert?
NEWTON. Nicht wahr, Sie ärgern sich, mich nicht verhaften zu dürfen?
INSPEKTOR. Aber Albert.
NEWTON. Möchten Sie mich verhaften, weil ich die Krankenschwester erdrosselt oder weil ich die Atombombe ermöglicht habe?
INSPEKTOR. Aber Albert.
NEWTON. Wenn Sie da neben der Türe den Schalter drehen, was geschieht, Richard?
INSPEKTOR. Das Licht geht an.
NEWTON. Sie stellen einen elektrischen Kontakt her. Verstehen Sie etwas von Elektrizität, Richard?
INSPEKTOR. Ich bin kein Physiker.
NEWTON. Ich verstehe auch wenig von ihr. Ich stelle nur auf Grund von Naturbeobachtungen eine Theorie über sie auf. Diese Theorie schreibe ich in der Sprache der Mathematik nieder und erhalte mehrere Formeln. Dann kommen die Techniker. Sie kümmern sich nur noch um die Formeln. Sie gehen mit der Elektrizität um wie der Zuhälter mit der Dirne. Sie nützen sie aus. Sie stellen Maschinen her, und brauchbar ist eine Maschine erst dann, wenn sie von der Erkenntnis unabhängig geworden ist, die zu ihrer Erfindung führte. So vermag heute jeder Esel eine Glühbirne zum Leuchten zu bringen — oder eine Atombombe zur Explosion.

(*Er klopft dem Inspektor auf die Schulter*)

Und nun wollen Sie mich dafür verhaften, Richard. Das ist nicht fair.

INSPEKTOR. Ich will Sie doch gar nicht verhaften, Albert.

NEWTON. Nur weil Sie mich für verrückt halten. Aber warum weigern Sie sich nicht, Licht anzudrehen, wenn Sie von Elektrizität nichts verstehen? Sie sind hier der Kriminelle, Richard. Doch nun muß ich meinen Kognak versorgen, sonst tobt die Oberschwester Marta Boll.

(*Newton versteckt*[1] *die Kognakflasche wieder hinter dem Kaminschirm,*[1] *läßt jedoch das Glas stehen*)

Leben Sie wohl.

INSPEKTOR. Leben Sie wohl, Albert.

NEWTON. Sie sollten sich selber verhaften, Richard!

(*Er verschwindet*[1] *wieder im Zimmer*[1] *Nummer 3*)

INSPEKTOR. Jetzt rauche ich einfach.

(*Er nimmt kurzentschlossen eine Zigarre aus seinem Etui, zündet sie an, raucht. Durch die Flügeltüre kommt Blocher*)

BLOCHER. Wir sind fahrbereit, Herr Inspektor.

(*Der Inspektor stampft auf den Boden*)

INSPEKTOR. Ich warte! Auf die Chefärztin!

BLOCHER. Jawohl, Herr Inspektor.

(*Der Inspektor beruhigt sich, brummt*)

---

[1] *versteckt ... hinter dem Kaminschirm ... verschwindet ... im Zimmer*: *verstecken*, to hide, *verschwinden*, to disappear, *erscheinen*, to appear, *ankommen*, to arrive, usually take a preposition + dative, but occasionally, especially with *verschwinden*, the accusative.

INSPEKTOR. Kehr mit der Mannschaft in die Stadt zurück, Blocher. Ich komme dann nach.
BLOCHER. Zu Befehl, Herr Inspektor.

(*Blocher ab*)
(*Der Inspektor pafft vor sich hin, erhebt sich, stapft trotzig im Salon herum, bleibt vor dem Porträt über dem Kamin stehen, betrachtet es. Inzwischen hat das Geigen und Klavierspiel aufgehört. Die Türe von Zimmer Nummer 2 öffnet sich und Fräulein Doktor Mathilde von Zahnd kommt heraus. Bucklig, etwa fünfundfünfzig, weißer Ärztemantel, Stethoskop*)

FRL. DOKTOR. Mein Vater, Geheimrat August von Zahnd. Er hauste in dieser Villa, bevor ich sie in ein Sanatorium umwandelte. Ein großer Mann, ein wahrer Mensch. Ich bin sein einziges Kind. Er haßte mich wie die Pest, er haßte überhaupt alle Menschen wie die Pest. Wohl mit Recht, als Wirtschaftsführer taten sich ihm menschliche Abgründe auf,[1] die uns Psychiatern auf ewig verschlossen sind. Wir Irrenärzte bleiben nun einmal hoffnungslos romantische Philanthropen.
INSPEKTOR. Vor drei Monaten hing ein anderes Porträt hier.
FRL. DOKTOR. Mein Onkel, der Politiker. Kanzler Joachim von Zahnd.

(*Sie legt die Partitur auf das Tischchen vor dem Sofa*)

FRL. DOKTOR. So. Ernesti hat sich beruhigt. Er warf sich aufs Bett und schlief ein. Wie ein glücklicher

---

[1] *taten sich ihm menschliche Abgründe auf*: deep abysses in human nature were revealed to him.

Bub. Ich kann wieder aufatmen. Ich befürchtete schon, er geige noch die dritte Brahmssonate.*

(*Sie setzt sich auf den Sessel links vom Sofa*)

INSPEKTOR. Entschuldigen Sie, Fräulein Doktor von Zahnd, daß ich hier verbotenerweise[1] rauche, aber —
FRL. DOKTOR. Rauchen Sie nur ruhig, Inspektor. Ich benötige auch dringend eine Zigarette, Oberschwester Marta hin oder her.[2] Geben Sie mir Feuer.

(*Er gibt ihr Feuer, sie raucht*)

Scheußlich. Die arme Schwester Irene. Ein blitzsauberes, junges Ding.

(*Sie bemerkt das Glas*)

Newton?
INSPEKTOR. Ich hatte das Vergnügen.
FRL. DOKTOR. Ich räume das Glas besser ab.

(*Der Inspektor kommt ihr zuvor[3] und stellt das Glas hinter das Kamingitter*)

Wegen der Oberschwester.
INSPEKTOR. Verstehe.
FRL. DOKTOR. Sie haben sich mit Newton unterhalten?
INSPEKTOR. Ich entdeckte etwas.

(*Er setzt sich aufs Sofa*)

FRL. DOKTOR. Gratuliere.
INSPEKTOR. Newton hält sich in Wirklichkeit auch für Einstein.

[1] *verbotenerweise*: against the rules, even though it is forbidden.
[2] *Oberschwester Marta hin oder her*: never mind sister Marta.
[3] *kommt ihr zuvor*: anticipates her action, does it first.

DIE PHYSIKER 17

Frl. Doktor. Das erzählt er jedem. In Wahrheit hält er sich aber doch[1] für Newton.
Inspektor (*verblüfft*). Sind Sie sicher?
Frl. Doktor. Für wen sich meine Patienten halten, bestimme ich. Ich kenne sie weitaus besser als sie sich selber kennen.
Inspektor. Möglich. Dann sollten Sie uns aber auch helfen, Fräulein Doktor. Die Regierung reklamiert.
Frl. Doktor. Der Staatsanwalt?
Inspektor. Tobt.
Frl. Doktor. Wie wenn das meine Sorge wäre, Voß.
Inspektor. Zwei Morde —
Frl. Doktor. Bitte, Inspektor.
Inspektor. Zwei Unglücksfälle. In drei Monaten. Sie müssen zugeben, daß die Sicherheitsmaßnahmen in Ihrer Anstalt ungenügend sind.
Frl. Doktor. Wie stellen Sie sich denn diese Sicherheitsmaßnahmen vor, Inspektor? Ich leite eine Heilanstalt, nicht ein Zuchthaus. Sie können schließlich die Mörder auch nicht einsperren, bevor sie morden.
Inspektor. Es handelt sich nicht um Mörder, sondern um Verrückte, und die können eben jederzeit morden.
Frl. Doktor. Gesunde auch und bedeutend öfters.[2] Wenn ich nur an meinen Großvater Leonidas von Zahnd denke, an den Generalfeldmarschall mit seinem verlorenen Krieg. In welchem Zeitalter leben wir denn? Hat die Medizin Fortschritte gemacht

---

[1] *doch*: after all, in spite of everything.
[2] *Gesunde auch und bedeutend öfters*: sane people too and much more often.

oder nicht? Stehen uns neue Mittel zur Verfügung[1] oder nicht, Drogen, die noch aus den Tobsüchtigsten sanfte Lämmer machen? Sollen wir die Kranken wieder in Einzelzellen sperren, womöglich noch in Netze mit Boxhandschuhen wie früher? Wie wenn wir nicht im Stande wären, gefährliche und ungefährliche Patienten zu unterscheiden.

INSPEKTOR. Dieses Unterscheidungsvermögen versagte jedenfalls bei Beutler und Ernesti kraß.[2]

FRL. DOKTOR. Leider. *Das* beunruhigt mich und nicht Ihr tobender Staatsanwalt.

(*Aus Zimmer Nummer 2 kommt Einstein mit seiner Geige. Hager, schlohweiße lange Haare, Schnurrbart*)

EINSTEIN. Ich bin aufgewacht.
FRL. DOKTOR. Aber, Professor.
EINSTEIN. Geigte ich schön?
FRL. DOKTOR. Wundervoll, Professor.
EINSTEIN. Ist Schwester Irene Straub —
FRL. DOKTOR. Denken Sie nicht mehr daran, Professor.
EINSTEIN. Ich gehe wieder schlafen.
FRL. DOKTOR. Das ist lieb, Professor.

(*Einstein zieht sich wieder auf sein Zimmer zurück. Der Inspektor ist aufgesprungen*)

INSPEKTOR. Das war er also!
FRL. DOKTOR. Ernst Heinrich Ernesti.
INSPEKTOR. Der Mörder —
FRL. DOKTOR. Bitte, Inspektor.

[1] *Stehen uns neue Mittel zur Verfügung ... ?*: have we new means at our disposal ... ?

[2] *Dieses Unterscheidungsvermögen versagte jedenfalls bei ... kraß*: this ability to discriminate failed utterly, however, in the case of. ...

DIE PHYSIKER

INSPEKTOR. Der Täter, der sich für Einstein hält. Wann wurde er eingeliefert?
FRL. DOKTOR. Vor zwei Jahren.
INSPEKTOR. Und Newton?
FRL. DOKTOR. Vor einem Jahr. Beide unheilbar. Voß, ich bin, weiß Gott, in meinem Métier keine Anfängerin, das ist Ihnen bekannt, und dem Staatsanwalt auch, er hat meine Gutachten immer geschätzt. Mein Sanatorium ist weltbekannt und entsprechend teuer. Fehler kann ich mir nicht leisten[1] und Vorfälle, die mir die Polizei ins Haus bringen, schon gar nicht. Wenn hier jemand versagte, so ist es die Medizin, nicht ich. Diese Unglücksfälle waren nicht vorauszusehen, ebenso gut könnten Sie oder ich Krankenschwestern erdrosseln. Es gibt medizinisch keine Erklärung für das Vorgefallene. Es sei denn[2]

(*Sie hat sich eine neue Zigarette genommen. Der Inspektor gibt ihr Feuer*)

Inspektor. Fällt Ihnen nichts auf?
INSPEKTOR. Inwiefern?
FRL. DOKTOR. Denken Sie an die beiden Kranken.
INSPEKTOR. Nun?
FRL. DOKTOR. Beide sind Physiker. Kernphysiker.
INSPEKTOR. Und?
FRL. DOKTOR. Sie sind wirklich ein Mensch ohne besonderen Argwohn, Inspektor.

(*Der Inspektor denkt nach*)

INSPEKTOR. Fräulein Doktor.

[1] *Fehler kann ich mir nicht leisten*: I can't afford mistakes.
[2] *Es sei denn (daß)*: unless.

FRL. DOKTOR. Voß?
INSPEKTOR. Sie glauben —?
FRL. DOKTOR. Beide untersuchten radioaktive Stoffe.
INSPEKTOR. Sie vermuten einen Zusammenhang?
FRL. DOKTOR. Ich stelle nur fest,[1] das ist alles. Beide werden wahnsinnig, bei beiden verschlimmert sich die Krankheit, beide werden gemeingefährlich,[2] beide erdrosseln Krankenschwestern.
INSPEKTOR. Sie denken an eine — Veränderung des Gehirns durch Radioaktivität?
FRL. DOKTOR. Ich muß diese Möglichkeit leider ins Auge fassen.[3]

(*Der Inspektor sieht sich um*)

INSPEKTOR. Wohin führt diese Türe?
FRL. DOKTOR. In die Halle, in den grünen Salon, zum oberen Stock.
INSPEKTOR. Wie viele Patienten befinden sich noch hier?
FRL. DOKTOR. Drei.
INSPEKTOR. Nur?
FRL. DOKTOR. Die übrigen wurden gleich nach dem ersten Unglücksfall in das neue Haus übergesiedelt. Ich hatte mir den Neubau zum Glück rechtzeitig leisten können. Reiche Patienten und auch meine Verwandten steuerten bei. Indem sie ausstarben. Meistens hier. Ich war dann Alleinerbin. Schicksal, Voß. Ich bin immer Alleinerbin. Meine Familie ist so alt, daß es beinahe einem kleinen medizinischen

---

[1] *Ich stelle nur fest*: I just state a fact.
[2] *gemeingefährlich*: a danger to everybody.
[3] *Ich muß . . . ins Auge fassen*: I must take into consideration. (This conversation anticipates the references made later to 'radioactive physicists'. Cf. note 1, p. 51.)

DIE PHYSIKER 21

Wunder gleichkommt, wenn ich relativ für normal
gelten darf,¹ ich meine, was meinen Geisteszustand
betrifft.²

(*Der Inspektor überlegt*)

INSPEKTOR. Der dritte Patient?
FRL. DOKTOR. Ebenfalls ein Physiker.
INSPEKTOR. Merkwürdig. Finden Sie nicht?
FRL. DOKTOR. Finde ich gar nicht. Ich sortiere. Die
Schriftsteller zu den Schriftstellern, die Großindus-
triellen zu den Großindustriellen, die Millionärinnen
zu den Millionärinnen und die Physiker zu den
Physikern.
INSPEKTOR. Name?
FRL. DOKTOR. Johann Wilhelm Möbius.*
INSPEKTOR. Hatte auch er mit Radioaktivität zu tun?
FRL. DOKTOR. Nichts.
INSPEKTOR. Könnte auch er — ?
FRL. DOKTOR. Er ist seit fünfzehn Jahren hier,³ harmlos,
und sein Zustand blieb unverändert.
INSPEKTOR. Fräulein Doktor. Sie kommen nicht darum
herum.⁴ Der Staatsanwalt verlangt für Ihre Physiker
kategorisch Pfleger.
FRL. DOKTOR. Er soll sie haben.

(*Der Inspektor greift nach seinem Hut*)

INSPEKTOR. Schön, es freut mich, daß Sie das einsehen.

¹ *es beinahe ... gelten darf*: it almost amounts to a medical miracle, if I can be considered relatively normal.
² *was ... betrifft*: as far as my mental condition is concerned.
³ *Er ist seit fünfzehn Jahren hier*: *has been* here for fifteen years. (For actions still continuing, *seit* + present tense renders the perfect tense in English, *seit* + imperfect renders the pluperfect in English.)
⁴ *Sie kommen nicht darum herum*: you won't get round it.

D

Ich war nun zweimal in Les Cerisiers, Fräulein Doktor von Zahnd. Ich hoffe nicht, noch einmal aufzutauchen.

(*Er setzt sich den Hut auf und geht links durch die Flügeltüre auf die Terrasse und entfernt sich durch den Park. Fräulein Doktor Mathilde von Zahnd sieht ihm nachdenklich nach. Von rechts kommt die Oberschwester Marta Boll, stutzt, schnuppert. In der Hand ein Dossier*)

OBERSCHWESTER. Bitte, Fräulein Doktor —
FRL. DOKTOR. Oh. Entschuldigen Sie.

(*Sie drückt die Zigarette aus*)

Ist Schwester Irene Straub aufgebahrt?[1]
OBERSCHWESTER. Unter der Orgel.
FRL. DOKTOR. Stellt Kerzen um sie und Kränze.
OBERSCHWESTER. Ich habe dem Blumen-Feuz[2] schon angeläutet.
FRL. DOKTOR. Wie geht es meiner Tante Senta?
OBERSCHWESTER. Unruhig.
FRL. DOKTOR. Dosis verdoppeln. Dem Vetter Ulrich?
OBERSCHWESTER. Stationär.
FRL. DOKTOR. Oberschwester Marta Boll: Ich muß mit einer Tradition von Les Cerisiers leider Schluß machen. Ich habe bis jetzt nur Krankenschwestern angestellt, morgen übernehmen Pfleger die Villa.
OBERSCHWESTER. Fräulein Doktor Mathilde von Zahnd: Ich lasse mir meine drei Physiker nicht rauben.[3] Sie sind meine interessantesten Fälle.

---

[1] *aufgebahrt*: laid out (*die Bahre* = bier).
[2] *Blumen-Feuz angeläutet*: rung up Feuz the florist.
[3] *Ich lasse mir ... nicht rauben*: I won't be robbed of. (Cf. note 1, p. 11.)

DIE PHYSIKER   23

FRL. DOKTOR.   Mein Entschluß ist endgültig.
OBERSCHWESTER.   Ich bin nur neugierig, woher Sie die Pfleger nehmen. Bei der heutigen Überbeschäftigung.
FRL. DOKTOR.   Das lassen Sie meine Sorge sein. Ist die Möbius gekommen?
OBERSCHWESTER.   Sie wartet im grünen Salon.
FRL. DOKTOR.   Ich lasse bitten.[1]
OBERSCHWESTER.   Die Krankheitsgeschichte Möbius.
FRL. DOKTOR.   Danke.

(*Die Oberschwester übergibt ihr das Dossier, geht dann zur Türe rechts hinaus, kehrt sich jedoch vorher noch einmal um*)

OBERSCHWESTER.   Aber —
FRL. DOKTOR.   Bitte, Oberschwester Marta, bitte.

(*Oberschwester ab. Frl. Doktor von Zahnd öffnet das Dossier, studiert es am runden Tisch. Von rechts führt die Oberschwester Frau Rose sowie drei Knaben von vierzehn, fünfzehn und sechzehn Jahren herein. Der Älteste trägt eine Mappe. Den Schluß bildet Missionar Rose.[2] Frl. Doktor erhebt sich*)

Meine liebe Frau Möbius —
FRAU ROSE.   Rose. Frau Missionar Rose. Ich muß Sie ganz grausam überraschen, Fräulein Doktor, aber ich habe vor drei Wochen Missionar Rose geheiratet. Vielleicht etwas eilig, wir lernten uns im September an einer Tagung kennen.

(*Sie errötet und weist etwas unbeholfen auf ihren neuen Mann*)

---
[1] *Ich lasse bitten*: ask her to come in.
[2] *Den Schluß bildet Missionar Rose*: Missionary Rose comes in last.

Oskar war Witwer.

(*Frl. Doktor schüttelt ihr die Hand*)

FRL. DOKTOR. Gratuliere, Frau Rose, gratuliere von ganzem Herzen. Und auch Ihnen, Herr Missionar, alles Gute.

(*Sie nickt ihm zu*)

FRAU ROSE. Sie verstehen unseren Schritt?

FRL. DOKTOR. Aber natürlich, Frau Rose. Das Leben hat weiterzublühen.

MISSIONAR ROSE. Wie still es hier ist! Wie freundlich. Ein wahrer Gottesfriede waltet in diesem Hause, so recht nach dem Psalmwort: Denn der Herr hört die Armen und verachtet seine Gefangenen nicht.[1]

FRAU ROSE. Oskar ist nämlich ein guter Prediger, Fräulein Doktor.

(*Sie errötet*)

Meine Buben.

FRL. DOKTOR. Grüß Gott, ihr Buben.

DIE DREI BUBEN. Grüß Gott, Fräulein Doktor.

(*Der Jüngste hat etwas vom Boden aufgenommen*)

JÖRG-LUKAS. Eine Lampenschnur, Fräulein Doktor. Sie lag auf dem Boden.

FRL. DOKTOR. Danke, mein Junge. Prächtige Buben, Frau Rose. Sie dürfen mit Vertrauen in die Zukunft blicken.

(*Frau Missionar Rose setzt sich aufs Sofa rechts, Frl. Doktor an den Tisch links. Hinter dem Sofa die drei Buben, auf dem Sessel rechts außen Missionar Rose*)

---

[1] *Psalmwort ... nicht*: see Psalms 69: 34.

DIE PHYSIKER 25

FRAU ROSE. Fräulein Doktor, ich bringe meine Buben nicht grundlos mit. Oskar übernimmt eine Missionsstation auf den Marianen.*

MISSIONAR ROSE. Im Stillen Ozean.

FRAU ROSE. Und ich halte es für schicklich, wenn meine Buben vor der Abreise ihren Vater kennenlernen. Zum ersten und letzten Mal. Sie waren ja noch klein, als er krank wurde und nun heißt es vielleicht Abschied für immer zu nehmen.

FRL. DOKTOR. Frau Rose, vom ärztlichen Standpunkte aus mögen sich zwar einige Bedenken melden,[1] aber menschlich finde ich Ihren Wunsch begreiflich und gebe die Bewilligung zu diesem Familientreffen gern.

FRAU ROSE. Wie geht es meinem Johann Wilhelmlein?

(Frl. Doktor blättert im Dossier)

FRL. DOKTOR. Unser guter Möbius macht weder Fort- noch Rückschritte, Frau Rose. Er puppt sich in sein Welt ein.

FRAU ROSE. Behauptet er immer noch, daß ihm der König Salomo* erscheine?

FRL. DOKTOR. Immer noch.

MISSIONAR ROSE. Eine traurige, beklagenswerte Verirrung.

FRL. DOKTOR. Ihr strammes Urteil erstaunt mich ein wenig, Herr Missionar Rose. Als Theologe müssen Sie doch immerhin mit der Möglichkeit eines Wunders rechnen.

[1] *mögen sich zwar einige Bedenken melden*: some scruples may be felt. (*Sich melden* = to announce oneself; *mögen* = (1) to like, (2) may, i.e. be possible; *zwar* followed by *aber* or *doch* in the next clause is approximately equivalent to a concessive clause beginning with *obgleich*, although.)

Missionar Rose. Selbstverständlich — aber doch nicht bei einem Geisteskranken.

Frl. Doktor. Ob die Erscheinungen, welche die Geisteskranken wahrnehmen, wirklich sind oder nicht, darüber hat die Psychiatrie, mein lieber Missionar Rose, nicht zu urteilen. Sie hat sich ausschließlich um den Zustand des Gemüts und der Nerven zu kümmern und da steht's bei unserem braven Möbius traurig genug, wenn auch[1] die Krankheit einen milden Verlauf nimmt. Helfen? Mein Gott! Eine Insulinkur wäre wieder einmal fällig gewesen, gebe ich zu, doch weil die anderen Kuren erfolglos verlaufen sind, ließ ich sie bleiben.[2] Ich kann leider nicht zaubern, Frau Rose, und unseren braven Möbius gesund päppeln,[3] aber quälen will ich ihn auch nicht.

Frau Rose. Weiß er, daß ich mich — ich meine, weiß er von der Scheidung?

Frl. Doktor. Er ist informiert.

Frau Rose. Begriff er?

Frl. Doktor. Er interessiert sich kaum mehr für die Außenwelt.

Frau Rose. Fräulein Doktor. Verstehen Sie mich recht. Ich bin fünf Jahre älter als Johann Wilhelm. Ich lernte ihn als fünfzehnjährigen Gymnasiasten im Hause meines Vaters kennen, wo er eine Mansarde gemietet hatte. Er war ein Waisenbub und bitter

---

[1] *da steht's ... traurig genug, wenn auch ...*: things look bad enough with our worthy Möbius, even though. . . .

[2] *weil die anderen Kuren ... ließ ich sie bleiben*: because the other treatments yielded no results, I didn't try this one.

[3] *gesund päppeln*: coddle back to health.

arm. Ich ermöglichte ihm das Abitur[1] und später das Studium der Physik. An seinem zwanzigsten Geburtstag haben wir geheiratet. Gegen den Willen meiner Eltern. Wir arbeiteten Tag und Nacht. Er schrieb seine Dissertation und ich übernahm eine Stelle in einem Transportgeschäft. Vier Jahre später kam Adolf-Friedrich, unser Ältester und dann die beiden andern Buben. Endlich stand eine Professur in Aussicht,[2] wir glaubten aufatmen zu dürfen, da wurde Johann Wilhelm krank und sein Leiden verschlang Unsummen. Ich trat in eine Schokoladefabrik ein, meine Familie durchzubringen. Bei Tobler.[3]

(*Sie wischt sich still eine Träne ab*)

Ein Leben lang mühte ich mich ab.

(*Alle sind ergriffen*)

FRL. DOKTOR. Frau Rose, Sie sind eine mutige Frau.
MISSIONAR ROSE. Und eine gute Mutter.
FRAU ROSE. Fräulein Doktor. Ich habe bis jetzt Johann Wilhelm den Aufenthalt in Ihrer Anstalt ermöglicht. Die Kosten gingen weit über meine Mittel, aber Gott half immer wieder. Doch nun bin ich finanziell erschöpft. Ich bringe das zusätzliche Geld nicht mehr auf.[4]

---

[1] *das Abitur*: the final school-leaving examination in German grammar schools.
[2] *Endlich stand ... in Aussicht*: at last there was a prospect of a professorship.
[3] *Bei Tobler*: at Tobler's (a Swiss manufacturer of chocolate products. A feature of Dürrenmatt's style is the rounding-off of long passages with very short phrases.)
[4] *bringe ... nicht mehr auf*: can't get together the additional money.

FRL. DOKTOR. Begreiflich, Frau Rose.
FRAU ROSE. Ich fürchte, Sie glauben nun, ich hätte Oskar nur geheiratet, um nicht mehr für Johann Wilhelm aufkommen zu müssen, Fräulein Doktor. Aber das stimmt nicht. Ich habe es jetzt noch schwerer. Oskar bringt sechs Buben in die Ehe mit.
FRL. DOKTOR. Sechs?
MISSIONAR ROSE. Sechs.
FRAU ROSE. Sechs. Oskar ist ein leidenschaftlicher Vater. Doch nun sind neun Kinder zu füttern und Oskar ist durchaus nicht robust,[1] seine Besoldung kärglich.

(*Sie weint*)

FRL. DOKTOR. Nicht doch Frau Rose, nicht doch. Keine Tränen.
FRAU ROSE. Ich mache mir die heftigsten Vorwürfe, mein armes Johann Wilhelmlein im Stich gelassen zu haben.
FRL. DOKTOR. Frau Rose! Sie brauchen sich nicht zu grämen.
FRAU ROSE. Johann Wilhelmlein wird jetzt sicher in einer staatlichen Heilanstalt interniert.
FRL. DOKTOR. Aber nein, Frau Rose. Unser braver Möbius bleibt hier in der Villa. Ehrenwort. Er hat sich eingelebt und liebe, nette Kollegen gefunden Ich bin schließlich kein Unmensch.
FRAU ROSE. Sie sind so gut zu mir, Fräulein Doktor.
FRL. DOKTOR. Gar nicht, Frau Rose, gar nicht. Es gibt nur Stiftungen. Der Oppelfond für kranke Wissenschaftler, die Doktor-Steinemann-Stiftung. Geld liegt

---

[1] *ein leidenschaftlicher Vater ... durchaus nicht robust*: The irony here is obvious.

wie Heu herum, und es ist meine Pflicht als Ärztin, Ihrem Johann Wilhelmlein davon etwas zuzuschaufeln.¹ Sie sollen mit einem guten Gewissen nach den Marianen dampfen dürfen. Aber nun wollen wir doch unseren guten Möbius mal herholen.

(*Sie geht nach dem Hintergrund und öffnet Türe Nummer 1. Frau Rose erhebt sich aufgeregt.*)

Lieber Möbius. Sie erhielten Besuch. Verlassen Sie Ihre Physikerklause² und kommen Sie.

(*Aus dem Zimmer Nummer 1 kommt Johann Wilhelm Möbius, ein vierzigjähriger, etwas unbeholfener Mensch. Er schaut sich unsicher im Zimmer um, betrachtet Frau Rose, dann die Buben, endlich Herrn Missionar Rose, scheint nichts zu begreifen, schweigt.*)

FRAU ROSE. Johann Wilhelm.
DIE BUBEN. Papi.

(*Möbius schweigt*)

FRL. DOKTOR. Mein braver Möbius, Sie erkennen mir doch noch Ihre Gattin wieder, hoffe ich.

(*Möbius starrt Frau Rose an*)

MÖBIUS. Lina?
FRL. DOKTOR. Es dämmert, Möbius. Natürlich ist es Ihre Lina.
MÖBIUS. Grüß dich, Lina.
FRAU ROSE. Johann Wilhelmlein, mein liebes, liebes Johann Wilhelmlein.

---

¹ *zuzuschaufeln*: to shovel some towards.
² *Physikerklause*: physicist's cubby-hole, den.

FRL. DOKTOR. So. Es wäre geschafft. Frau Rose, Herr Missionar, wenn Sie mich noch zu sprechen wünschen, stehe ich drüben im Neubau zur Verfügung.

(*Sie geht durch die Flügeltüre links ab*)

FRAU ROSE. Deine Buben, Johann Wilhelm.

(*Möbius stutzt*)

MÖBIUS. Drei?
FRAU ROSE. Aber natürlich, Johann Wilhelm. Drei.

(*Sie stellt ihm die Buben vor*)

Adolf-Friedrich, dein Ältester.

(*Möbius schüttelt ihm die Hand*)

MÖBIUS. Freut mich, Adolf-Friedrich, mein Ältester.
ADOLF-FRIEDRICH. Grüß dich, Papi.
MÖBIUS. Wie alt bist du denn, Adolf-Friedrich?
ADOLF-FRIEDRICH. Sechzehn, Papi.
MÖBIUS. Was willst du werden?
ADOLF-FRIEDRICH. Pfarrer, Papi.
MÖBIUS. Ich erinnere mich. Ich führte dich einmal an der Hand über den Sankt-Josephsplatz. Die Sonne schien grell und die Schatten waren wie abgezirkelt.[1]

(*Möbius wendet sich zum nächsten*)

Und du — du bist?
WILFRIED-KASPAR. Ich heiße Wilfried-Kaspar, Papi.
MÖBIUS. Vierzehn?
WILFRIED-KASPAR. Fünfzehn. Ich möchte Philosophie studieren.

---

[1] *wie abgezirkelt*: sharply defined (as if measured with compasses; *der Zirkel* = pair of compasses. Ill makes a similar remark in *Der Besuch der alten Dame*.)

MÖBIUS. Philosophie?
FRAU ROSE. Ein besonders frühreifes Kind.
WILFRIED-KASPAR. Ich habe Schopenhauer und Nietzsche[1] gelesen.
FRAU ROSE. Dein Jüngster, Jörg-Lukas. Vierzehnjährig.
JÖRG-LUKAS. Grüß dich, Papi.
MÖBIUS. Grüß dich, Jörg-Lukas, mein Jüngster.
FRAU ROSE. Er gleicht dir am meisten.
JÖRG-LUKAS. Ich will ein Physiker werden, Papi.

(*Möbius starrt seinen Jüngsten erschrocken an*)

MÖBIUS. Physiker?
JÖRG-LUKAS. Jawohl, Papi.
MÖBIUS. Das darfst du nicht, Jörg-Lukas. Keinesfalls. Das schlage dir aus dem Kopf. Ich — ich verbiete es dir.

(*Jörg-Lukas ist verwirrt*)

JÖRG-LUKAS. Aber du bist doch auch ein Physiker geworden, Papi —
MÖBIUS. Ich hätte es nie werden dürfen,[2] Jorg-Lukas. Nie. Ich wäre jetzt nicht im Irrenhaus.
FRAU ROSE. Aber Johann Wilhelm, das ist doch ein Irrtum. Du bist in einem Sanatorium, nicht in einem Irrenhaus. Deine Nerven sind einfach angegriffen, das ist alles.

---

[1] *Schopenhauer und Nietzsche*: leading German philosophers of the nineteenth century.

[2] *Ich hätte es nie werden dürfen*: I should never have been allowed to become one. (In the perfect and pluperfect tenses the *infinitive* of the modal auxiliary verbs is used as a past participle if the modal auxiliary verb governs another infinitive form; here *ich hätte* = I should have, *dürfen* = been allowed, *werden* = to become.)

(*Möbius schüttelt den Kopf*)

MÖBIUS. Nein, Lina. Man hält mich für verrückt. Alle. Auch du. Und auch meine Buben. Weil mir der König Salomo erscheint.

(*Alle schweigen verlegen. Frau Rose stellt Missionar Rose vor*)

FRAU ROSE. Hier stelle ich dir Oskar Rose vor, Johann Wilhelm. Meinen Mann. Er ist Missionar.
MÖBIUS. Dein Mann? Aber ich bin doch dein Mann.
FRAU ROSE. Nicht mehr, Johann Wilhelmlein.

(*Sie errötet*)

Wir sind doch geschieden.
MÖBIUS. Geschieden?
FRAU ROSE. Das weißt du doch.
MÖBIUS. Nein.
FRAU ROSE. Fräulein Doktor von Zahnd teilte es dir mit. Ganz bestimmt.
MÖBIUS. Möglich.
FRAU ROSE. Und dann heiratete ich eben Oskar. Er hat sechs Buben. Er war Pfarrer in Guttannen und hat nun eine Stelle auf den Marianen angenommen.
MÖBIUS. Auf den Marianen?
MISSIONAR ROSE. Im Stillen Ozean.
FRAU ROSE. Wir schiffen uns übermorgen in Bremen ein.
MÖBIUS. Ach so.

(*Er starrt Missionar Rose an. Alle sind verlegen*)

FRAU ROSE. Ja. So ist es eben.

(*Möbius nickt Missionar Rose zu*)

MÖBIUS. Es freut mich, den neuen Vater meiner Buben kennenzulernen, Herr Missionar.

MISSIONAR ROSE. Ich habe sie fest in mein Herz geschlossen, Herr Möbius, alle drei. Gott wird uns helfen, nach dem Psalmwort: Der Herr ist mein Hirte, mir wird nichts mangeln.

FRAU ROSE. Oskar kennt alle Psalmen auswendig. Die Psalmen Davids, die Psalmen Salomos.

MÖBIUS. Ich bin froh, daß die Buben einen tüchtigen Vater gefunden haben. Ich bin ein ungenügender Vater gewesen.

(*Die drei Buben protestieren*)

DIE BUBEN. Aber nein, Papi.

MÖBIUS. Und auch Lina hat einen würdigeren Gatten gefunden.

FRAU ROSE. Aber Johann Wilhelmlein.

MÖBIUS. Ich gratuliere von ganzem Herzen.

FRAU ROSE. Wir müssen bald aufbrechen.

MÖBIUS. Nach den Marianen.

FRAU ROSE. Abschied voneinander nehmen.

MÖBIUS. Für immer.

FRAU ROSE. Deine Buben sind bemerkenswert musikalisch, Johann Wilhelm. Sie spielen sehr begabt Blockflöte.[1] Spielt eurem Papi zum Abschied etwas vor, Buben.

DIE BUBEN. Jawohl, Mami.

(*Adolf-Friedrich öffnet die Mappe, verteilt die Blockflöten*)

FRAU ROSE. Nimm Platz, Johann Wilhelmlein.

[1] *Blockflöte* (f.): recorder.

(*Möbius nimmt am runden Tisch Platz. Frau Rose und Missionar Rose setzen sich aufs Sofa. Die Buben stellen sich in der Mitte des Salons auf.*)

JÖRG-LUKAS. Etwas von Buxtehude.*
ADOLF-FRIEDRICH. Eins, zwei, drei.

(*Die Buben spielen Blockflöte*)

FRAU ROSE. Inniger, Buben, inniger.*

(*Die Buben spielen inniger. Möbius springt auf*)

MÖBIUS. Lieber nicht! Bitte, lieber nicht!

(*Die Buben halten verwirrt inne*)

Spielt nicht weiter. Bitte. Salomo zuliebe. Spielt nicht weiter.
FRAU ROSE. Aber Johann Wilhelm!
MÖBIUS. Bitte, nicht mehr spielen. Bitte, nicht mehr spielen. Bitte, bitte.
MISSIONAR ROSE. Herr Möbius. Gerade der König Salomo wird sich über das Flötenspiel dieser unschuldigen Knaben freuen. Denken Sie doch: Salomo, der Psalmdichter, Salomo, der Sänger des Hohen Liedes!*
MÖBIUS. Herr Missionar. Ich kenne Salomo von Angesicht zu Angesicht. Er ist nicht mehr der große goldene König, der Sulamith besingt, und die Rehzwillinge,* die unter Rosen weiden, er hat seinen Purpurmantel von sich geworfen (*Möbius eilt mit einem Male an der erschrockenen Familie vorbei*[1] *nach hinten zu*

---

[1] *eilt mit einem Male an der erschrockenen Familie vorbei*: hurries all at once past the frightened family (*an* + dative + *vorbei* = past).

seinem Zimmer und reißt die Türe auf), nackt und
stinkend kauert er in meinem Zimmer als der arme
König der Wahrheit, und seine Psalmen sind
schrecklich. Hören Sie gut zu, Missionar, Sie lieben
Psalmworte, kennen sie alle, lernen Sie auch die
auswendig:

(*Er ist zum runden Tisch links gegangen, kehrt ihn um,
steigt in ihn hinein, sitzt in ihn*)[1]

Ein Psalm Salomos, den Weltraumfahrern zu singen[2]

Wir hauten ins Weltall ab*
Zu den Wüsten des Monds. Versanken in ihrem
    Staub
Lautlos verreckten
Manche schon da. Doch die meisten verkochten
In den Bleidämpfen des Merkur, lösten sich auf
In den Ölpfützen der Venus und
Sogar auf dem Mars fraß uns die Sonne
Donnernd, radioaktiv und gelb

Jupiter stank
Ein pfeilschnell rotierender Methanbrei[3]
Hing er so mächtig über uns
Daß wir Ganymed vollkotzten

FRAU ROSE. Aber Johann Wilhelm —

---

[1] *sitzt in ihn*: one would expect 'setzt sich in ih*n*' or 'sitzt in ihm'.
[2] *den Weltraumfahrern zu singen*: to be sung to the space-travellers.
(Cf. note 1, p. 11.)
[3] *Methanbrei*: methane pulp. (Methane, a common gas, is a constituent of Jupiter's atmosphere.)

FRIEDRICH DÜRRENMATT

MÖBIUS.

> Saturn bedachten wir mit Flüchen[1]
> Was dann weiter kam, nicht der Rede wert[2]
>
> Uranus Neptun
> Graugrünlich, erfroren
> Über Pluto und Transpluto[3] fielen die letzten
> Unanständigen Witze.
>
> Hatten wir doch längst die Sonne mit Sirius verwechselt
> Sirius mit Kanopus
>
> Abgetrieben trieben wir in die Tiefen hinauf[4]
> Einigen weißen Sternen zu
> Die wir gleichwohl nie erreichten
>
> Längst schon Mumien in unseren Schiffen
> Verkrustet von Unflat
>
> In den Fratzen kein Erinnern mehr
> An die atmende Erde

OBERSCHWESTER. Aber, aber Herr Möbius!

[1] *bedachten wir mit Flüchen*: we supplied with curses. (*Bedenken mit* often has a tinge of irony, e.g. *er bedachte den Hund mit einem Fußtritt*: he gave the dog a kick.)

[2] *nicht der Rede wert*: not worth mentioning (*wert* + preceding genitive).

[3] *Transpluto*: Pluto is the furthest known planet in the solar system, but some astronomers believe there may be another planet beyond this.

[4] *in die Tiefen hinauf*: up into the depths. (This suggests the infinity of space.)

(*Die Oberschwester hat mit Schwester Monika von rechts den Raum betreten. Möbius sitzt starr, das Gesicht maskenhaft, im umgekehrten Tisch*)

MÖBIUS. Packt euch nun nach den Marianen fort!¹
FRAU ROSE. Johann Wilhelmlein —
DIE BUBEN. Papi —
MÖBIUS. Packt euch fort! Schleunigst! Nach den Marianen!

(*Er erhebt sich drohend. Die Familie Rose ist verwirrt*)

OBERSCHWESTER. Kommt, Frau Rose, kommt ihr Buben und Herr Missionar. Er muß sich beruhigen, das ist alles.
MÖBIUS. Hinaus mit euch! Hinaus!
OBERSCHWESTER. Ein leichter Anfall. Schwester Monika wird bei ihm bleiben, wird ihn beruhigen. Ein leichter Anfall.
MÖBIUS. Schiebt ab!² Für immer! Nach dem Stillen Ozean!
JÖRG-LUKAS. Adieu Papi! Adieu!

(*Die Oberschwester führt die bestürzte und weinende Familie nach rechts hinaus. Möbius schreit ihnen hemmungslos nach*)

MÖBIUS. Ich will euch nie mehr sehen! Ihr habt den König Salomo beleidigt! Ihr sollt verflucht sein! Ihr sollt mit den ganzen Marianen im Marianengraben* versaufen! Elftausend Meter tief. Im

---

¹ *Packt euch ... fort!*: Clear off to ... !
² *Schiebt ab!*: push off!

schwärzesten Loch des Meeres sollt ihr verfaulen, von Gott vergessen und den Menschen!

SCHWESTER MONIKA. Wir sind allein. Ihre Familie hört Sie nicht mehr.

(*Möbius starrt Schwester Monika verwundert an, scheint sich endlich zu finden*)

MÖBIUS. Ach so, natürlich.

(*Schwester Monika schweigt. Er ist etwas verlegen*)

Ich war wohl etwas heftig?
SCHWESTER MONIKA. Ziemlich.
MÖBIUS. Ich mußte die Wahrheit sagen.
SCHWESTER MONIKA. Offenbar.
MÖBIUS. Ich regte mich auf.
SCHWESTER MONIKA. Sie verstellten sich.[1]
MÖBIUS. Sie durchschauten mich?
SCHWESTER MONIKA. Ich pflege Sie nun zwei Jahre.

(*Er geht auf und ab, bleibt dann stehen*)

MÖBIUS. Gut. Ich gebe es zu. Ich spielte den Wahnsinnigen.
SCHWESTER MONIKA. Weshalb?
MÖBIUS. Um von meiner Frau Abschied zu nehmen und von meinen Buben. Abschied für immer.
SCHWESTER MONIKA. Auf diese schreckliche Weise?
MÖBIUS. Auf diese humane Weise. Die Vergangenheit löscht man am besten mit einem wahnsinnigen Betragen aus, wenn man sich schon im Irrenhaus befindet: Meine Familie kann mich nun mit gutem Gewissen vergessen. Mein Auftritt hat ihr die Lust

[1] *Sie verstellten sich*: you were pretending, putting on an act.

genommen, mich noch einmal aufzusuchen. Die Folgen meinerseits sind unwichtig, nur das Leben außerhalb der Anstalt zählt. Verrücktsein kostet.[1] Fünfzehn Jahre zahlte meine gute Lina bestialische Summen, ein Schlußstrich mußte endlich gezogen werden.[2] Der Augenblick war günstig. Salomo hat mir offenbart, was zu offenbaren war, das System aller möglichen Erfindungen* ist abgeschlossen, die letzten Seiten sind diktiert, und meine Frau hat einen neuen Gatten gefunden, den kreuzbraven Missionar Rose. Sie dürfen beruhigt sein, Schwester Monika. Es ist nun alles in Ordnung.

(*Er will abgehen*)

SCHWESTER MONIKA. Sie handelten planmäßig.
MÖBIUS. Ich bin Physiker.

(*Er wendet sich seinem Zimmer zu*)

SCHWESTER MONIKA. Herr Möbius.

(*Er bleibt stehen*)

MÖBIUS. Schwester Monika?
SCHWESTER MONIKA. Ich habe mit Ihnen zu reden.
MÖBIUS. Bitte.
SCHWESTER MONIKA. Es geht um uns beide.[3]
MÖBIUS. Nehmen wir Platz.

(*Sie setzen sich. Sie aufs Sofa, er auf den Sessel links davon*)

---

[1] *Verrückstein kostet*: being mad is expensive.
[2] *ein Schlußstrich mußte endlich gezogen werden*: finally an end had to be made to it.
[3] *Es geht um uns beide*: it concerns both of us.

SCHWESTER MONIKA. Auch wir müssen von einander Abschied nehmen. Auch für immer.

(*Er erschrickt*)

MÖBIUS. Sie verlassen mich?
SCHWESTER MONIKA. Befehl.
MÖBIUS. Was ist geschehen?
SCHWESTER MONIKA. Man versetzt mich ins Hauptgebäude. Morgen übernehmen hier Pfleger die Bewachung. Eine Krankenschwester darf diese Villa nicht mehr betreten.
MÖBIUS. Newtons und Einsteins wegen?
SCHWESTER MONIKA. Auf Verlangen des Staatsanwalts. Die Chefärztin befürchtete Schwierigkeiten und gab nach.

(*Schweigen. Er ist niedergeschlagen*)

MÖBIUS. Schwester Monika, ich bin unbeholfen. Ich verlernte es, Gefühle auszudrücken, die Fachsimpeleien mit den beiden Kranken, neben denen ich lebe, sind ja kaum Gespräche zu nennen. Ich bin verstummt, ich fürchte, auch innerlich. Doch Sie sollen wissen, daß für mich alles anders geworden ist, seit ich Sie kenne. Erträglicher. Nun, auch diese Zeit ist vorüber. Zwei Jahre, in denen ich etwas glücklicher war als sonst. Weil ich durch Sie, Schwester Monika, den Mut gefunden habe, meine Abgeschlossenheit und mein Schicksal als — Verrückter — auf mich zu nehmen. Leben Sie wohl.

(*Er steht auf und will ihr die Hand reichen*)

SCHWESTER MONIKA. Herr Möbius, ich halte Sie nicht für — verrückt.

DIE PHYSIKER   41

(Möbius lacht, setzt sich wieder)

MÖBIUS. Ich mich auch nicht. Aber das ändert nichts an meiner Lage. Ich habe das Pech, daß mir der König Salomo erscheint. Es gibt nun einmal nichts anstößigeres als ein Wunder im Reiche der Wissenschaft.

SCHWESTER MONIKA. Herr Möbius, ich glaube an dieses Wunder.

(Möbius starrt sie fassungslos an)

MÖBIUS. Sie glauben?
SCHWESTER MONIKA. An den König Salomo.
MÖBIUS. Daß er mir erscheint?
SCHWESTER MONIKA. Daß er Ihnen erscheint.
MÖBIUS. Jeden Tag, jede Nacht?
SCHWESTER MONIKA. Jeden Tag, jede Nacht.
MÖBIUS. Daß er mir die Geheimnisse der Natur diktiert? Den Zusammenhang aller Dinge? Das System aller möglichen Erfindungen?
SCHWESTER MONIKA. Ich glaube daran. Und wenn Sie erzählten, auch noch der König David erscheine Ihnen mit seinem Hofstaat, würde ich es glauben. Ich weiß einfach, daß Sie nicht krank sind. Ich fühle es.

(Stille. Dann springt Möbius auf)

MÖBIUS. Schwester Monika! Gehen Sie!

(Sie bleibt sitzen)

SCHWESTER MONIKA. Ich bleibe.
MÖBIUS. Ich will Sie nie mehr sehen.
SCHWESTER MONIKA. Sie haben mich nötig. Sie haben sonst niemand mehr auf der Welt. Keinen Menschen.

MÖBIUS. Es ist tödlich, an den König Salomo zu glauben.
SCHWESTER MONIKA. Ich liebe Sie.

(*Möbius starrt Schwester Monika ratlos an, setzt sich wieder. Stille*)

MÖBIUS (*leise, niedergeschlagen*). Sie rennen in Ihr Verderben.
SCHWESTER MONIKA. Ich fürchte nicht für mich, ich fürchte für Sie. Newton und Einstein sind gefährlich.
MÖBIUS. Ich komme mit ihnen aus.[1]
SCHWESTER MONIKA. Auch Schwester Dorothea und Schwester Irene kamen mit ihnen aus. Und dann kamen sie um.
MÖBIUS. Schwester Monika. Sie haben mir Ihren Glauben und Ihre Liebe gestanden. Sie zwingen mich, Ihnen nun auch die Wahrheit zu sagen. Ich liebe Sie ebenfalls, Monika.

(*Sie starrt ihn an*)

MÖBIUS. Mehr als mein Leben. Und darum sind Sie in Gefahr. Weil wir uns lieben.

(*Aus Zimmer Nummer 2 kommt Einstein, raucht eine Pfeife*)

EINSTEIN. Ich bin wieder aufgewacht.
SCHWESTER MONIKA. Aber Herr Professor.
EINSTEIN. Ich erinnerte mich plötzlich.
SCHWESTER MONIKA. Aber Herr Professor.
EINSTEIN. Ich erdrosselte Schwester Irene.
SCHWESTER MONIKA. Denken Sie nicht mehr daran, Herr Professor.

[1] *Ich komme mit ihnen aus*: I get on with them quite well.

(*Er betrachtet seine Hände*)

EINSTEIN. Ob ich noch jemals fähig bin, Geige zu spielen?

(*Möbius erhebt sich, wie um Monika zu schützen*)

MÖBIUS. Sie geigten ja schon wieder.
EINSTEIN. Passabel?
MÖBIUS. Die Kreutzersonate. Während die Polizei da war.
EINSTEIN. Die Kreutzersonate. Gott sei Dank.

(*Seine Miene hat sich aufgeklärt, verdüstert sich aber wieder*)

Dabei geige ich gar nicht gern und die Pfeife liebe ich auch nicht. Sie schmeckt scheußlich.
MÖBIUS. Dann lassen Sie es sein.
EINSTEIN. Kann ich doch nicht. Als Albert Einstein.

(*Er schaut die beiden scharf an*)

Ihr liebt einander?
SCHWESTER MONIKA. Wir lieben uns.

(*Einstein geht nachdenklich hinaus in den Hintergrund wo die ermordete Schwester lag*)

EINSTEIN. Auch Schwester Irene und ich liebten uns. Sie wollte alles für mich tun, die Schwester Irene. Ich warnte sie. Ich schrie sie an. Ich behandelte sie wie einen Hund. Ich flehte sie an, zu fliehen. Vergeblich. Sie blieb. Sie wollte mit mir aufs Land ziehen. Nach Kohlwang. Sie wollte mich heiraten. Sogar die Bewilligung hatte sie schon. Von Fräulein Doktor von Zahnd. Da erdrosselte ich sie. Die arme Schwester Irene. Es gibt nichts unsinnigeres auf der Welt als die Raserei, mit der sich die Weiber aufopfern.

(*Schwester Monika geht zu ihm*)

SCHWESTER MONIKA. Legen Sie sich wieder hin, Professor.
EINSTEIN. Sie dürfen mich Albert nennen.
SCHWESTER MONIKA. Seien Sie vernünftig, Albert.
EINSTEIN. Seien Sie vernünftig, Schwester Monika. Gehorchen Sie Ihrem Geliebten und fliehen Sie! Sonst sind Sie verloren.

(*Er wendet sich wieder dem Zimmer Nummer 2 zu*)

Ich gehe wieder schlafen.

(*Er verschwindet in Nummer 2*)

SCHWESTER MONIKA. Dieser arme irre Mensch.
MÖBIUS. Er sollte Sie endlich von der Unmöglichkeit überzeugt haben, mich zu lieben.
SCHWESTER MONIKA. Sie sind nicht verrückt.
MÖBIUS. Es wäre vernünftiger, Sie hielten mich dafür. Fliehen Sie! Machen Sie sich aus dem Staube! Hauen Sie ab![1] Sonst muß ich Sie auch noch wie einen Hund behandeln.
SCHWESTER MONIKA. Behandeln Sie mich lieber wie eine Geliebte.
MÖBIUS. Kommen Sie, Monika.

(*Er führt sie zu einem Sessel, setzt sich ihr genenüber, ergreift ihre Hände*)

Hören Sie zu. Ich habe einen schweren Fehler

---

[1] *Machen Sie sich aus dem Staube! Hauen Sie ab!*: Get out of here! Off with you!

begangen. Ich habe mein Geheimnis verraten, ich habe Salomos Erscheinen nicht verschwiegen. Dafür läßt er mich büßen. Lebenslänglich. In Ordnung. Aber Sie sollen nicht auch noch dafür bestraft werden. In den Augen der Welt lieben Sie einen Geisteskranken. Sie laden nur Unglück auf sich. Verlassen Sie die Anstalt, vergessen Sie mich. So ist es am besten für uns beide.

SCHWESTER MONIKA. Begehren Sie mich?

MÖBIUS. Warum reden Sie so mit mir?

SCHWESTER MONIKA. Ich will mit Ihnen schlafen, ich will Kinder von Ihnen haben. Ich weiß, ich rede schamlos. Aber warum schauen Sie mich nicht an? Gefalle ich Ihnen denn nicht? Ich gebe zu, meine Schwesterntracht ist gräßlich.

(Sie reißt sich die Haube vom Haar)

Ich hasse meinen Beruf! Fünf Jahre habe ich nun die Kranken gepflegt, im Namen der Nächstenliebe. Ich habe mein Gesicht nie abgewendet, ich war für alle da, ich habe mich aufgeopfert. Aber nun will ich mich für jemanden allein aufopfern, für jemanden allein dasein, nicht immer für andere. Ich will für meinen Geliebten dasein. Für Sie. Ich will alles tun, was Sie von mir verlangen, für Sie arbeiten Tag und Nacht, nur fortschicken dürfen Sie mich nicht! Ich habe doch auch niemanden mehr auf der Welt als Sie! Ich bin doch auch allein!

MÖBIUS. Monika. Ich muß Sie fortschicken.

SCHWESTER MONIKA *(verzweifelt)*. Lieben Sie mich denn gar nicht?

MÖBIUS. Ich liebe Sie, Monika. Mein Gott, ich liebe

Sie, das ist ja das Wahnsinnige.

SCHWESTER MONIKA. Warum verraten Sie mich dann? Und nicht nur mich? Sie behaupten, der König Salomo erscheine Ihnen. Warum verraten Sie auch ihn?

(*Möbius ungeheuer erregt, packt sie*)

MÖBIUS. Monika! Sie dürfen alles von mir glauben, mich für einen Schwächling halten. Ihr Recht. Ich bin unwürdig Ihrer Liebe. Aber Salomo bin ich treu geblieben. Er ist in mein Dasein eingebrochen, auf einmal, ungerufen, er hat mich mißbraucht, mein Leben zerstört, aber ich habe ihn nicht verraten.

SCHWESTER MONIKA. Sind Sie sicher?

MÖBIUS. Sie zweifeln?

SCHWESTER MONIKA. Sie glauben, dafür büßen zu müssen, weil Sie sein Erscheinen nicht verschwiegen haben. Aber vielleicht büßen Sie dafür, weil Sie sich für seine Offenbarung nicht einsetzen.[1]

(*Er läßt sie fahren*)[2]

MÖBIUS. Ich — verstehe Sie nicht.

SCHWESTER MONIKA. Er diktiert Ihnen das System aller möglichen Erfindungen. Kämpften Sie für seine Anerkennung?

MÖBIUS. Man hält mich doch für verrückt.

SCHWESTER MONIKA. Warum sind Sie so mutlos?

MÖBIUS. Mut ist in meinem Falle ein Verbrechen.

SCHWESTER MONIKA. Johann Wilhelm. Ich sprach mit Fräulein Doktor von Zahnd.

---

[1] *weil Sie sich für seine Offenbarung nicht einsetzen*: because you do nothing to help his revelation. (*Sich einsetzen für* = work actively on behalf of.)

[2] *Er läßt sie fahren*: he lets her go, leaves hold of her.

(*Möbius starrt sie an*)

MÖBIUS. Sie sprachen?
SCHWESTER MONIKA. Sie sind frei.
MÖBIUS. Frei?
SCHWESTER MONIKA. Wir dürfen uns heiraten.
MÖBIUS. Mein Gott.
SCHWESTER MONIKA. Fräulein Doktor von Zahnd hat schon alles geregelt. Sie hält Sie zwar für krank, aber für ungefährlich. Und für erblich nicht belastet.[1] Sie selbst sei verrückter als Sie, erklärte sie und lachte.[2]
MÖBIUS. Das ist lieb von ihr.
SCHWESTER MONIKA. Ist sie nicht ein prächtiger Mensch?
MÖBIUS. Sicher.
SCHWESTER MONIKA. Johann Wilhelm! Ich habe den Posten einer Gemeindeschwester in Blumenstein angenommen. Ich habe gespart. Wir brauchen uns nicht zu sorgen. Wir brauchen uns nur richtig lieb zu haben.

(*Möbius hat sich erhoben. Im Zimmer wird es allmählich dunkel*)

Ist es nicht wunderbar?
MÖBIUS. Gewiß.
SCHWESTER MONIKA. Sie freuen sich nicht.

[1] *Sie hält Sie ... für erblich nicht belastet*: she does not think you have any hereditary complaints. (*Halten für* = consider as, take for. For *zwar* see note 1, p. 25.)

[2] *Sie selbst sei verrückter als Sie, erklärte sie und lachte*: The irony of this remark is intended to anticipate the part played by the Fräulein Doktor at the end of the second act; cf. Einstein, p. 82: 'Sie sind verrückt!'

Möbius. Es kommt so unerwartet.
Schwester Monika. Ich habe noch mehr getan.
Möbius. Das wäre?
Schwester Monika. Mit dem berühmten Physiker Professor Scherbert gesprochen.
Möbius. Er war mein Lehrer.
Schwester Monika. Er erinnerte sich genau. Sie seien sein bester Schüler gewesen.
Möbius. Und was besprachen Sie mit ihm?
Schwester Monika. Er versprach mir, Ihre Manuskripte unvoreingenommen zu prüfen.
Möbius. Erklärten Sie auch, daß sie von Salomo stammen?
Schwester Monika. Natürlich.
Möbius. Und?
Schwester Monika. Er lachte. Sie seien immer ein toller Spaßvogel gewesen.[1] Johann Wilhelm! Wir haben nicht nur an uns zu denken. Sie sind auserwählt. Salomo ist Ihnen erschienen, offenbarte sich Ihnen in seinem Glanz, die Weisheit des Himmels wurde Ihnen zuteil. Nun haben Sie den Weg zu gehen, den das Wunder befiehlt, unbeirrbar, auch wenn der Weg durch Spott und Gelächter führt, durch Unglauben und Zweifel. Aber er führt aus dieser Anstalt. Johann Wilhelm, er führt in die Öffentlichkeit, nicht in die Einsamkeit, er führt in den Kampf. Ich bin da, dir zu helfen, mit dir zu kämpfen, der Himmel, der dir Salomo schickte, schickte auch mich.

(*Möbius starrt zum Fenster hinaus*)

[1] *Sie seien immer ... gewesen*: he said you'd always been a great joker.

DIE PHYSIKER 49

Liebster.
MÖBIUS. Geliebte?
SCHWESTER MONIKA. Bist du nicht froh?
MÖBIUS. Sehr.
SCHWESTER MONIKA. Wir müssen nun deine Koffer packen. Acht Uhr zwanzig geht der Zug. Nach Blumenstein.
MÖBIUS. Viel ist ja nicht.[1]
SCHWESTER MONIKA. Es ist dunkel geworden.
MÖBIUS. Die Nacht kommt jetzt früh.
SCHWESTER MONIKA. Ich mache Licht.
MÖBIUS. Warte noch. Komm zu mir.

(*Sie geht zu ihm. Nur noch die beiden Silhouetten sind sichtbar*)

SCHWESTER MONIKA. Du hast Tränen in den Augen.
MÖBIUS. Du auch.
SCHWESTER MONIKA. Vor Glück.*

(*Er reißt den Vorhang herunter und über sie. Kurzer Kampf. Die Silhouetten sind nicht mehr sichtbar. Dann Stille. Die Türe von Zimmer Nummer 3 öffnet sich. Ein Lichtstrahl dringt in den Raum. Newton steht in der Türe im Kostüm seines Jahrhunderts. Möbius erhebt sich*)

NEWTON. Was ist geschehen?
MÖBIUS. Ich habe Schwester Monika Stettler erdrosselt.

(*Aus Zimmer Nummer 2 hört man Einstein geigen*)

NEWTON. Da geigt Einstein wieder. Kreisler.* Schön Rosmarin.*

(*Er geht zum Kamin, holt den Kognak*)

[1] *Viel ist ja nicht*: there isn't much (to pack).

ZWEITER AKT

Eine Stunde später. Der gleiche Raum. Draussen Nacht. Wieder Polizei. Wieder messen, aufzeichnen, photographieren. Nur ist jetzt die für das Publikum unsichtbare Leiche der Monika Stettler hinten rechts unter dem Fenster anzunehmen. Der Salon ist erleuchtet. Der Lüster brennt, die Stehlampe. Auf dem Sofa sitzt Frl. Doktor Mathilde von Zahnd, düster, in sich versunken. Auf dem kleinen Tisch vor ihr eine Zigarrenkiste, auf dem Sessel rechts außen Guhl mit Stenoblock. Inspektor Voß wendet sich in Hut und Mantel von der Leiche ab, kommt nach vorne.

FRL. DOKTOR. Eine Havanna?
INSPEKTOR. Nein, danke.
FRL. DOKTOR. Schnaps?
INSPEKTOR. Später.

(Schweigen)

Blocher, du kannst jetzt photographieren.*
BLOCHER. Jawohl, Herr Inspektor.

(Man photographiert. Blitzlichter)

INSPEKTOR. Wie hieß die Schwester?*
FRL. DOKTOR. Monika Stettler.
INSPEKTOR. Alter?
FRL. DOKTOR. Fünfundzwanzig. Aus Blumenstein.
INSPEKTOR. Angehörige?
FRL. DOKTOR. Keine.
INSPEKTOR. Haben Sie die Aussagen, Guhl?
GUHL. Jawohl, Herr Inspektor.

DIE PHYSIKER

INSPEKTOR. Auch erdrosselt, Doktor?
GERICHTSMEDIZINER. Eindeutig. Wieder mit Riesenkräften. Nur diesmal mit der Vorhangkordel.
INSPEKTOR. Wie vor drei Monaten.

(*Er setzt sich müde auf den Sessel rechts vorne*)

FRL. DOKTOR. Möchten Sie nun den Mörder —*
INSPEKTOR. Bitte, Fräulein Doktor.
FRL. DOKTOR. Ich meine, den Täter sehen?
INSPEKTOR. Ich denke nicht daran.
FRL. DOKTOR. Aber —
INSPEKTOR. Fräulein Doktor von Zahnd. Ich tue meine Pflicht, nehme Protokoll, besichtige die Leiche, lasse sie photographieren und durch unseren Gerichtsmediziner begutachten, aber Möbius besichtige ich nicht. Den überlasse ich Ihnen. Endgültig. Mit den andern radioaktiven Physikern.¹
FRL. DOKTOR. Der Staatsanwalt?
INSPEKTOR. Tobt nicht einmal mehr. Brütet.

(*Sie wischt sich den Schweiß ab*)

FRL. DOKTOR. Heiß hier.
INSPEKTOR. Durchaus nicht.
FRL. DOKTOR. Dieser dritte Mord —
INSPEKTOR. Bitte, Fräulein Doktor.
FRL. DOKTOR. Dieser dritte Unglücksfall* hat mir in Les Cerisiers gerade noch gefehlt.² Ich kann abdanken. Monika Stettler war meine beste Pflegerin. Sie verstand die Kranken. Sie konnte sich einfühlen. Ich liebte sie wie eine Tochter. Aber ihr

---

¹ *Mit den andern radioaktiven Physikern*: Cf. note 3, p. 20.
² *hat mir . . . gerade noch gefehlt*: was the last straw. (*Fehlen* + dative = to be lacking.)

Tod ist noch nicht das schlimmste. Mein medizinischer Ruf ist dahin.¹

INSPEKTOR. Der kommt schon wieder.² Blocher, mache noch eine Aufnahme von oben.

BLOCHER. Jawohl, Herr Inspektor.

(*Von rechts schieben zwei riesenhafte Pfleger* einen Wagen mit Geschirr und Essen herein. Einer der Pfleger ist ein Neger. Sie sind von einem ebenso riesenhaften Oberpfleger begleitet.*)

OBERPFLEGER. Das Abendbrot für die lieben Kranken, Fräulein Doktor.

(*Der Inspektor springt auf*)

INSPEKTOR. Uwe Sievers.

OBERPFLEGER. Richtig, Herr Inspektor. Uwe Sievers. Ehemaliger Europameister im Schwergewichtsboxen. Nun Oberpfleger in Les Cerisiers.

INSPEKTOR. Und die zwei andern Ungeheuer?

OBERPFLEGER. Murillo, südamerikanischer Meister, auch im Schwergewicht, und McArthur (*er zeigt auf den Neger*), nordamerikanischer Meister, Mittelgewicht. Stell den Tisch auf, McArthur.

(*McArthur stellt den Tisch auf*)

Das Tischtuch, Murillo.

(*Murillo breitet ein weißes Tuch über den Tisch*)

Das Meißnerporzellan,*³ McArthur.

¹ *Mein ... dahin*: my reputation as a doctor is ruined.
² *Der kommt schon wieder*: that (i.e. your reputation as a doctor) will soon come back again. (The definite article is often used as a demonstrative pronoun: 'that one', 'he', etc.)
³ *Das Meißnerporzellan*: Dresden china. (See note, p. 101.)

(*McArthur verteilt das Geschirr*)

Das Silberbesteck, Murillo.

(*Murillo verteilt das Besteck*)

Die Suppenschüssel in die Mitte, McArthur.

(*McArthur stellt die Suppenschüssel auf den Tisch*)

INSPEKTOR. Was kriegen denn unsere lieben Kranken?

(*Er hebt den Deckel der Suppenschüssel hoch*)

Leberknödelsuppe.[1]
OBERPFLEGER. Poulet à la broche,[2] Cordon bleu.[3]
INSPEKTOR. Fantastisch.
OBERPFLEGER. Erste Klasse.
INSPEKTOR. Ich bin ein Beamter vierzehnter Klasse,[4] da geht's zu Hause weniger kulinarisch zu.[5]
OBERPFLEGER. Es ist angerichtet,[6] Fräulein Doktor.
FRL. DOKTOR. Sie können gehen, Sievers. Die Patienten bedienen sich selbst.
OBERPFLEGER. Herr Inspektor, wir hatten die Ehre.

(*Die drei verbeugen sich und gehen nach rechts hinaus.
Der Inspektor sieht ihnen nach*)

INSPEKTOR. Donnerwetter.

[1] *Leberknödelsuppe*: a soup made with dumplings and liver.
[2] *Poulet à la broche*: chicken roasted on the spit.
[3] *Cordon bleu*: name of a celebrated French school of cookery; hence, a first-rate cook. Here, a dish made from veal, ham, and cheese.
[4] *vierzehnter Klasse* (genitive): fourteenth grade. (This implies that his salary is very modest.)
[5] *da geht's zu Hause weniger kulinarisch zu*: at my home the cuisine is much simpler.
[6] *Es ist angerichtet*: the table is laid.

FRL. DOKTOR. Zufrieden?
INSPEKTOR. Neidisch. Wenn wir die bei der Polizei hätten —
FRL. DOKTOR. Die Gagen sind astronomisch.
INSPEKTOR. Mit Ihren Schlotbaronen und Multimillionärinnen können Sie sich das ja leisten. Die Burschen werden den Staatsanwalt endlich beruhigen. Denen entkommt niemand.

(*Im Zimmer Nummer 2 hört man Einstein geigen*)

Und auch Einstein geigt wieder.
FRL. DOKTOR. Kreisler. Wie meistens. Liebesleid.*
BLOCHER. Wir wären fertig, Herr Inspektor.
INSPEKTOR. Dann schafft die Leiche wieder mal hinaus.

(*Zwei Polizisten heben die Leiche hoch. Da stürzt Möbius aus Zimmer Nummer 1*)

MÖBIUS. Monika! Meine Geliebte!

(*Die Polizisten mit der Leiche bleiben stehen. Fräulein Doktor erhebt sich majestätisch*)

FRL. DOKTOR. Möbius! Wie konnten Sie das tun? Sie haben meine beste Krankenschwester getötet, meine sanfteste Krankenschwester, meine süßeste Krankenschwester!
MÖBIUS. Es tut mir ja so leid, Fräulein Doktor.
FRL. DOKTOR. Leid.
MÖBIUS. König Salomo befahl es.
FRL. DOKTOR. Der König Salomo.

(*Sie setzt sich wieder. Schwerfällig. Bleich*)

Seine Majestät ordnete den Mord an.

MÖBIUS. Ich stand am Fenster und starrte in den dunklen Abend. Da schwebte der König vom Park her über die Terrasse ganz nahe an mich heran¹ und flüsterte mir durch die Scheibe den Befehl zu.
FRL. DOKTOR. Entschuldigen Sie, Voß. Meine Nerven.
INSPEKTOR. Schon in Ordnung.
FRL. DOKTOR. So eine Anstalt reibt auf.²
INSPEKTOR. Kann ich mir denken.
FRL. DOKTOR. Ich ziehe mich zurück.

(*Sie erhebt sich*)

Herr Inspektor Voß: Drücken Sie dem Staatsanwalt mein Bedauern über die Vorfälle in meinem Sanatorium aus. Versichern Sie ihm, es sei nun alles in Ordnung. Herr Gerichtsmediziner, meine Herren, ich hatte die Ehre.

(*Sie geht zuerst nach hinten links, verneigt sich vor der Leiche, feierlich, schaut dann Möbius an, geht dann nach rechts hinaus*)

INSPEKTOR. So. Nun könnt ihr die Leiche endgültig in die Kapelle tragen. Zu Schwester Irene.
MÖBIUS. Monika!

(*Die beiden Polizisten mit der Leiche, die andern mit den Apparaten durch die Gartentüre ab. Der Gerichtsmediziner folgt*)

Meine geliebte Monika.

(*Der Inspektor tritt zum kleinen Tischchen beim Sofa*)

---

¹ *schwebte . . . ganz nahe an mich heran*: came quite close up to me in hovering flight.

² *So eine Anstalt reibt auf*: such an institution is very wearing, gets on one's nerves.

INSPEKTOR. Jetzt benötige ich doch eine Havanna. Ich habe sie verdient.

(*Nimmt eine riesige Zigarre aus der Kiste, betrachtet sie*)

Tolles Ding.¹

(*Beißt sie an, zündet sie an*)

Mein lieber Möbius, hinter dem Kamingitter ist Sir Isaak Newtons Kognak versteckt.
MÖBIUS. Bitte, Herr Inspektor.

(*Der Inspektor pafft vor sich hin, während Möbius die Kognakflasche und das Glas holt*)

Darf ich einschenken?
INSPEKTOR. Sie dürfen.

(*Er nimmt das Glas, trinkt*)

MÖBIUS. Noch einen?
INSPEKTOR. Noch einen.

(*Möbius schenkt wieder ein*)

MÖBIUS. Herr Inspektor, ich muß Sie bitten, mich zu verhaften.
INSPEKTOR. Aber wozu denn, mein lieber Möbius?
MÖBIUS. Weil ich doch die Schwester Monika —
INSPEKTOR. Nach Ihrem eigenen Geständnis haben Sie auf Befehl des Königs Salomo gehandelt. So lange ich den nicht verhaften kann, bleiben Sie frei.
MÖBIUS. Trotzdem —
INSPEKTOR. Es gibt kein trotzdem. Schenken Sie mir noch einmal ein.

¹ *Tolles Ding*: enormous thing (i.e. the cigar; *toll* normally means 'mad', 'crazy').

MÖBIUS. Bitte, Herr Inspektor.
INSPEKTOR. Und nun versorgen Sie den Kognak wieder, sonst saufen ihn die Pfleger aus.
MÖBIUS. Jawohl, Herr Inspektor.

(*Er versorgt den Kognak*)

INSPEKTOR. Sehen Sie, ich verhafte jährlich im Städtchen und in der Umgebung einige Mörder. Nicht viele. Kaum ein Halbdutzend. Einige verhafte ich mit Vergnügen, andere tun mir leid. Aber ich muß sie trotzdem verhaften. Die Gerechtigkeit ist die Gerechtigkeit. Und nun kommen Sie und Ihre zwei Kollegen. Zuerst habe ich mich ja geärgert, daß ich nicht einschreiten durfte, doch jetzt? Ich genieße es auf einmal. Ich könnte jubeln. Ich habe drei Mörder gefunden, die ich mit gutem Gewissen nicht zu verhaften brauche. Die Gerechtigkeit macht zum ersten Male Ferien, ein immenses Gefühl. Die Gerechtigkeit, mein Freund, strengt nämlich mächtig an,[1] man ruiniert sich in ihrem Dienst, gesundheitlich und moralisch, ich brauche einfach eine Pause. Mein Lieber, diesen Genuß verdanke ich Ihnen. Leben Sie wohl. Grüßen Sie mir Newton und Einstein recht freundlich und lassen Sie mich bei Salomo empfehlen.[2]
MÖBIUS. Jawohl, Herr Inspektor.

(*Der Inspektor geht ab. Möbius ist allein. Er setzt sich auf das Sofa, preßt mit den Händen seine Schläfen. Aus Zimmer Nummer 3 kommt Newton.*)

NEWTON. Was gibt es denn?

---

[1] *strengt nämlich mächtig an*: is, you see, very strenuous. (*nämlich* = you know, you see, for.)
[2] *lassen Sie mich bei . . . empfehlen*: give my kind regards to. . . .

(*Möbius schweigt. Newton deckt die Suppenschüssel auf*)

Leberknödelsuppe.

(*Deckt die anderen Speisen auf dem Wagen auf*)

Poulet à la broche, Cordon bleu. Merkwürdig. Sonst essen wir doch abends leicht. Und bescheiden. Seit die andern Patienten im Neubau sind.

(*Er serviert sich Suppe*)

Keinen Hunger?

(*Möbius schweigt*)

Verstehe. Nach meiner Krankenschwester verging mir auch der Appetit.[1]

(*Er setzt sich und beginnt Leberknödelsuppe zu essen. Möbius erhebt sich und will auf sein Zimmer gehen*)

Bleiben Sie.
MÖBIUS. Sir Isaak?
NEWTON. Ich habe mit Ihnen zu reden, Möbius.

(*Möbius bleibt stehen*)

MÖBIUS. Und?

(*Newton deutet auf das Essen*)

NEWTON. Möchten Sie nicht vielleicht doch die Leberknödelsuppe versuchen? Sie schmeckt vorzüglich.
MÖBIUS. Nein.
NEWTON. Mein lieber Möbius, wir werden nicht mehr von Schwestern betreut, wir werden von Pflegern bewacht. Von riesigen Burschen.

[1] *verging mir auch der Appetit*: I also lost my appetite.

MÖBIUS. Das spielt doch keine Rolle.¹
NEWTON. Vielleicht nicht für Sie, Möbius. Sie wünschen ja offenbar Ihr ganzes Leben im Irrenhaus zu verbringen. Aber für mich spielt es eine Rolle. Ich will nämlich hinaus.

(*Er beendet die Leberknödelsuppe*)

Na. Gehen wir mal zum Poulet à la broche über.

(*Er serviert sich*)

Die Pfleger zwingen mich zu handeln. Noch heute.
MÖBIUS. Ihre Sache.
NEWTON. Nicht ganz. Ein Geständnis, Möbius: Ich bin nicht verrückt.
MÖBIUS. Aber natürlich nicht, Sir Isaak.
NEWTON. Ich bin nicht Sir Isaak Newton.
MÖBIUS. Ich weiß. Albert Einstein.
NEWTON. Blödsinn. Auch nicht Herbert Georg Beutler, wie man hier glaubt. Mein wahrer Name lautet Kilton, mein Junge.

(*Möbius starrt ihn erschrocken an*)

MÖBIUS. Alec Jasper Kilton?
NEWTON. Richtig.
MÖBIUS. Der Begründer der Entsprechungslehre?²*
NEWTON. Der.

(*Möbius kommt zum Tisch*)

MÖBIUS. Sie haben sich hier eingeschlichen?
NEWTON. Indem ich den Verrückten spielte.

¹ *spielt keine Rolle*: is unimportant.
² *Entsprechungslehre* (f.): theory of correspondences. (See note, p. 102.)

Möbius. Um mich — auszuspionieren?

Newton. Um hinter den Grund Ihrer Verrücktheit zu kommen. Mein tadelloses Deutsch ist mir im Lager unseres Geheimdienstes beigebracht worden, eine schreckliche Arbeit.

Möbius. Und weil die arme Schwester Dorothea auf die Wahrheit kam, haben Sie —

Newton. Habe ich. Der Vorfall tut mir außerordentlich leid.

Möbius. Verstehe.*

Newton. Befehl ist Befehl.

Möbius. Selbstverständlich.

Newton. Ich durfte nicht anders handeln.

Möbius. Natürlich nicht.

Newton. Meine Mission stand in Frage, das geheimste Unternehmen unseres Geheimdienstes. Ich mußte töten, wollte ich jeden Verdacht vermeiden. Schwester Dorothea hielt mich nicht mehr für verrückt, die Chefärztin nur für mäßig erkrankt, es galt meinen Wahnsinn durch einen Mord endgültig zu beweisen.[1] Sie, das Poulet à la broche schmeckt aber wirklich großartig.

(*Aus Zimmer Nummer 2 hört man Einstein geigen*)

Möbius. Da geigt Einstein wieder.

Newton. Die Gavotte von Bach.*

Möbius. Sein Essen wird kalt.

Newton. Lassen Sie den Verrückten ruhig weitergeigen.

Möbius. Eine Drohung?

---

[1] *es galt ... endgültig zu beweisen*: it was a question of proving once and for all.

NEWTON. Ich verehre Sie unermeßlich. Es würde mir leid tun, energisch vorgehen zu müssen.[1]

MÖBIUS. Sie haben den Auftrag, mich zu entführen?

NEWTON. Falls sich der Verdacht unseres Geheimdienstes bestätigt.

MÖBIUS. Der wäre?

NEWTON. Er hält Sie zufällig für den genialsten Physiker der Gegenwart.

MÖBIUS. Ich bin ein schwer nervenkranker Mensch, Kilton, nichts weiter.

NEWTON. Unser Geheimdienst ist darüber anderer Ansicht.

MÖBIUS. Und was glauben Sie von mir?

NEWTON. Ich halte Sie schlicht für den größten Physiker aller Zeiten.

MÖBIUS. Und wie kam Ihr Geheimdienst auf meine Spur?

NEWTON. Durch mich. Ich las zufällig Ihre Dissertation über die Grundlagen einer neuen Physik. Zuerst hielt ich die Abhandlung für eine Spielerei. Dann fiel es mir wie Schuppen von den Augen. Ich hatte es mit dem genialsten Dokument der neueren Physik zu tun. Ich begann über den Verfasser nachzuforschen und kam nicht weiter. Darauf informierte ich den Geheimdienst und der kam dann weiter.

EINSTEIN. Sie waren nicht der einzige Leser der Dissertation, Kilton.

(*Er ist unbemerkt mit seiner Geige unter dem Arm und mit seinem Geigenbogen aus Zimmer Nummer 2 erschienen*)

---

[1] *energisch vorgehen zu müssen*: to have to take energetic action.

Ich bin nämlich auch nicht verrückt. Darf ich mich vorstellen? Ich bin ebenfalls Physiker. Mitglied eines Geheimdienstes. Aber eines ziemlich anderen. Mein Name ist Joseph Eisler.

MÖBIUS. Der Entdecker des Eisler-Effekts?*
EINSTEIN. Der.
NEWTON. Neunzehnhundertfünfzig verschollen.
EINSTEIN. Freiwillig.

(*Newton hält plötzlich einen Revolver in der Hand*)

NEWTON. Darf ich bitten, Eisler, sich mit dem Gesicht gegen die Wand zu stellen?
EINSTEIN. Aber natürlich.

(*Er schlendert gemächlich zum Kamin, legt seine Geige auf das Kaminsims, kehrt sich dann plötzlich um, einen Revolver in der Hand*)

Mein bester Kilton. Da wir beide, wie ich vermute, mit Waffen tüchtig umzugehen wissen, wollen wir doch ein Duell möglichst vermeiden, finden Sie nicht? Ich lege meinen Browning gern zur Seite, falls Sie auch Ihren Colt —

NEWTON. Einverstanden.
EINSTEIN. Hinter das Kamingitter zum Kognak. Im Falle, es kämen plötzlich die Pfleger.
NEWTON. Schön.

(*Beide legen ihre Revolver hinter das Kamingitter*)

EINSTEIN. Sie brachten meine Pläne durcheinander, Kilton. Sie hielt ich wirklich für verrückt.
NEWTON. Trösten Sie sich: Ich Sie auch.
EINSTEIN. Überhaupt ging manches schief. Die Sache mit der Schwester Irene zum Beispiel heute nach-

mittag. Sie hatte Verdacht geschöpft, und damit war ihr Todesurteil gefällt. Der Vorfall tut mir außerordentlich leid.

MÖBIUS. Verstehe.
EINSTEIN. Befehl ist Befehl.
MÖBIUS. Selbstverständlich.
EINSTEIN. Ich konnte nicht anders handeln.
MÖBIUS. Natürlich nicht.
EINSTEIN. Auch meine Mission stand in Frage, das geheimste Unternehmen auch meines Geheimdienstes. Setzen wir uns?
NEWTON. Setzen wir uns.

(*Er setzt sich links an den Tisch, Einstein rechts*)

MÖBIUS. Ich nehme an, Eisler, auch Sie wollen mich nun zwingen —
EINSTEIN. Aber Möbius.
MÖBIUS. — bewegen, Ihr Land aufzusuchen.
EINSTEIN. Auch wir halten Sie schließlich für den größten aller Physiker. Aber nun bin ich auf das Abendessen gespannt. Die reinste Henkersmahlzeit.*

(*Er schöpft sich Suppe*)

Immer noch keinen Appetit, Möbius?
MÖBIUS. Doch. Plötzlich. Jetzt, wo ihr dahintergekommen seid.

(*Er setzt sich zwischen die beiden an den Tisch, schöpft sich ebenfalls Suppe*)

NEWTON. Burgunder, Möbius?
MÖBIUS. Schenken Sie ein.

(*Newton schenkt ein*)

NEWTON. Ich nehme das Cordon bleu in Angriff.¹
MÖBIUS. Tun Sie sich keinen Zwang an.²
NEWTON. Mahlzeit.³
EINSTEIN. Mahlzeit.
MÖBIUS. Mahlzeit.

(*Sie essen. Von rechts kommen die drei Pfleger, der Oberpfleger mit Notizbuch*)

OBERPFLEGER. Patient Beutler!
NEWTON. Hier.
OBERPFLEGER. Patient Ernesti!
EINSTEIN. Hier.
OBERPFLEGER. Patient Möbius!
MÖBIUS. Hier.
OBERPFLEGER. Oberpfleger Sievers, Pfleger Murillo, Pfleger McArthur.

(*Er steckt das Notizbuch wieder ein*)

OBERPFLEGER. Auf Anraten der Behörde sind gewisse Sicherheitsmaßnahmen zu treffen. Murillo, die Gitter zu.

(*Murillo läßt beim Fenster ein Gitter⁴ herunter. Der Raum hat nun auf einmal etwas von einem Gefängnis*)

McArthur, schließ ab.

(*McArthur schließt das Gitter ab*)

Haben die Herren für die Nacht noch einen Wunsch? Patient Beutler?

---

¹ *Ich nehme . . . in Angriff*: I'll tackle, set about.
² *Tun Sie sich keinen Zwang an*: don't hold yourself back, eat as much as you feel like. (*Zwang* (m.) = compulsion, restraint.)
³ *Mahlzeit*: short for *Gesegnete Mahlzeit*, usually said before a meal.
⁴ *Gitter* (n.): iron or steel grille.

NEWTON. Nein.
OBERPFLEGER. Patient Ernesti?
EINSTEIN. Nein.
OBERPFLEGER. Patient Möbius?
MÖBIUS. Nein.
OBERPFLEGER. Meine Herren. Wir empfehlen uns.[1] Gute Nacht.

(*Die drei Pfleger ab. Stille*)

EINSTEIN. Biester.
NEWTON. Im Park lauern noch weitere Kolosse. Ich habe sie längst von meinem Fenster aus beobachtet.

(*Einstein erhebt sich und untersucht das Gitter*)

EINSTEIN. Solid. Mit einem Spezialschloß.

(*Newton geht zu seiner Zimmertüre, öffnet sie, schaut hinein*)

NEWTON. Auch vor meinem Fenster mit einem Mal ein Gitter. Wie hingezaubert.[2]

(*Er öffnet die beiden andern Türen im Hintergrund*)

Auch bei Eisler. Und bei Möbius.

(*Er geht zur Türe rechts*)

Abgeschlossen.

(*Er setzt sich wieder. Auch Einstein*)

EINSTEIN. Gefangen.
NEWTON. Logisch. Wir mit unseren Krankenschwestern.

[1] *Wir empfehlen uns*: we take our leave.
[2] *Wie hingezaubert*: as if put there by magic.

Einstein. Jetzt kommen wir nur noch aus dem Irrenhaus, wenn wir gemeinsam vorgehen.[1]

Möbius. Ich will ja gar nicht fliehen.

Einstein. Möbius —

Möbius. Ich finde nicht den geringsten Grund dazu. Im Gegenteil. Ich bin mit meinem Schicksal zufrieden.

(*Schweigen*)

Newton. Doch ich bin nicht damit zufrieden, ein ziemlich entscheidender Umstand, finden Sie nicht? Ihre persönlichen Gefühle in Ehren,[2] aber Sie sind ein Genie und als solches Allgemeingut. Sie drangen in neue Gebiete der Physik vor. Aber Sie haben die Wissenschaft nicht gepachtet. Sie haben die Pflicht, die Türe auch uns aufzuschließen, den Nicht-Genialen. Kommen Sie mit mir, in einem Jahr stecken wir Sie in einen Frack, transportieren Sie nach Stockholm und Sie erhalten den Nobelpreis.*

Möbius. Ihr Geheimdienst ist uneigennützig.

Newton. Ich gebe zu, Möbius, daß ihn vor allem die Vermutung beeindruckt, Sie hätten das Problem der Gravitation gelöst.

Möbius. Stimmt.[3]

(*Stille*)

Einstein. Das sagen Sie so seelenruhig?

Möbius. Wie soll ich es denn sonst sagen?

Einstein. Mein Geheimdienst glaubte, Sie würden die

---

[1] *wenn wir gemeinsam vorgehen*: if we take joint action.

[2] *Ihre persönlichen Gefühle in Ehren*: all honour to your personal feelings.

[3] *Stimmt*: = *es stimmt*, (it is) correct.

DIE PHYSIKER 67

einheitliche Theorie der Elementarteilchen —¹
MÖBIUS. Auch Ihren Geheimdienst kann ich beruhigen. Die einheitliche Feldtheorie* ist gefunden.

(*Newton wischt sich mit der Serviette den Schweiß von der Stirne*)

NEWTON. Die Weltformel.²
EINSTEIN. Zum Lachen. Da versuchen Horden gut besoldeter Physiker in riesigen staatlichen Laboratorien seit Jahren³ vergeblich in der Physik weiterzukommen, und Sie erledigen das en passant⁴ im Irrenhaus am Schreibtisch.

(*Er wischt sich ebenfalls mit der Serviette den Schweiß von der Stirne*)

NEWTON. Und das System aller möglichen Erfindungen, Möbius?
MÖBIUS. Gibt es auch. Ich stellte es aus Neugierde auf, als praktisches Kompendium zu meinen theoretischen Arbeiten. Soll ich den Unschuldigen spielen? Was wir denken, hat seine Folgen. Es war meine Pflicht, die Auswirkungen zu studieren, die meine Feldtheorie und mein Gravitationslehre haben würden. Das Resultat ist verheerend. Neue, unvorstellbare Energien würden freigesetzt und eine Technik ermöglicht,

---

¹ *die einheitliche Theorie der Elementarteilchen*: the uniform theory of elementary particles.
² *Die Weltformel*: the world formula. (A universal formula explaining all aspects of science.)
³ *versuchen Horden gut besoldeter Physiker ... seit Jahren*: hordes of well-paid physicists have been trying for years. (For tense with *seit* see note 3, p. 21.)
⁴ *en passant*: by the way, casually.

die jeder Fantasie spottet,¹ falls meine Untersuchung in die Hände der Menschen fiele.

EINSTEIN. Das wird sich kaum vermeiden lassen.

NEWTON. Die Frage ist nur, wer zuerst an sie herankommt.²

(*Möbius lacht*)

MÖBIUS. Sie wünschen dieses Glück wohl Ihrem Geheimdienst, Kilton, und dem Generalstab, der dahinter steht?

NEWTON. Warum nicht? Um den größten Physiker aller Zeiten in die Gemeinschaft der Physiker zurückzuführen, ist mir jeder Generalstab heilig. Es geht um die Freiheit unserer Wissenschaft³ und um nichts weiter. Wer diese Freiheit garantiert, ist gleichgültig. Ich diene jedem System, läßt mich das System in Ruhe.⁴ Ich weiß, man spricht heute von der Verantwortung der Physiker. Wir haben es auf einmal mit der Furcht zu tun⁵ und werden moralisch. Das ist Unsinn. Wir haben Pionierarbeit zu leisten und nichts außerdem. Ob die Menschheit den Weg zu gehen versteht, den wir ihr bahnen, ist ihre Sache, nicht die unsrige.

EINSTEIN. Zugegeben. Wir haben Pionierarbeit zu leisten. Das ist auch meine Meinung. Doch dürfen

---

¹ *die jeder Fantasie spottet*: which scoffs at, is beyond the realms of, the imagination.

² *wer zuerst an sie herankommt*: who gets hold of it first.

³ *Es geht um die Freiheit unserer Wissenschaft*: the freedom of our science is at stake.

⁴ *läßt mich das System in Ruhe*: if the system leaves me in peace. ('If' can be rendered by putting the verb first.)

⁵ *Wir haben es auf einmal mit der Furcht zu tun*: all at once we get afraid.

wir die Verantwortung nicht ausklammern. Wir liefern der Menschheit gewaltige Machtmittel. Das gibt uns das Recht, Bedingungen zu stellen. Wir müssen Machtpolitiker werden, weil wir Physiker sind. Wir müssen entscheiden, zu wessen Gunsten wir unsere Wissenschaft anwenden, und ich habe mich entschieden. Sie dagegen sind ein jämmerlicher Ästhet,* Kilton. Warum kommen Sie dann nicht zu uns, wenn Ihnen nur an der Freiheit der Wissenschaft gelegen ist?[1] Auch wir können es uns schon längst nicht mehr leisten, die Physiker zu bevormunden. Auch wir brauchen Resultate. Auch unser politisches System muß der Wissenschaft aus der Hand fressen.

NEWTON. Unsere beiden politischen Systeme, Eisler, müssen jetzt vor allem Möbius aus der Hand fressen.

EINSTEIN. Im Gegenteil. Er wird uns gehorchen müssen. Wir beide halten ihn schließlich in Schach.

NEWTON. Wirklich? Wir beide halten wohl mehr uns in Schach. Unsere Geheimdienste sind leider auf die gleiche Idee gekommen. Machen wir uns doch nichts vor.[2] Überlegen wir doch die unmögliche Lage, in die wir dadurch geraten sind. Geht Möbius mit Ihnen, kann ich nichts dagegen tun, weil Sie es verhindern würden. Und Sie wären hilflos, wenn sich Möbius zu meinen Gunsten entschlösse.[3] Er kann hier wählen, nicht wir.

(Einstein erhebt sich feierlich)

[1] *wenn Ihnen nur an der Freiheit der Wissenschaft gelegen ist*: if you are only concerned about the freedom of science.
[2] *Machen wir uns doch nichts vor*: let us not deceive ourselves.
[3] *wenn sich Möbius zu meinen Gunsten entschlösse*: if Möbius were to decide in my favour. (*entschlösse* is the imperfect subjunctive.)

EINSTEIN. Holen wir die Revolver.

(*Newton erhebt sich ebenfalls*)

NEWTON. Kämpfen wir.

(*Newton holt die beiden Revolver hinter dem Kamingitter, gibt Einstein dessen Waffe*)

EINSTEIN. Es tut mir leid, daß die Angelegenheit ein blutiges Ende findet. Aber wir müssen schießen. Auf einander und auf die Wärter ohnehin. Im Notfall auch auf Möbius. Er mag der wichtigste Mann der Welt sein,[1] seine Manuskripte sind wichtiger.

MÖBIUS. Meine Manuskripte? Ich habe sie verbrannt.

(*Totenstille*)

EINSTEIN. Verbrannt?

MÖBIUS (*verlegen*). Vorhin. Bevor die Polizei zurückkam. Um sicher zu gehen.

(*Einstein bricht in ein verzweifeltes Gelächter aus*)

EINSTEIN. Verbrannt.

(*Newton schreit wütend auf*)

NEWTON. Die Arbeit von fünfzehn Jahren.

EINSTEIN. Es ist zum wahnsinnig werden.

NEWTON. Offiziell sind wir es ja schon.

(*Sie stecken ihre Revolver ein und setzen sich vernichtet aufs Sofa*)

EINSTEIN. Damit sind wir Ihnen endgültig ausgeliefert, Möbius.

[1] *Er mag ... sein*: he may be. (Cf. note 1, p. 25.)

DIE PHYSIKER 71

NEWTON. Und dafür mußte ich eine Krankenschwester erdrosseln und Deutsch lernen.

EINSTEIN. Während man mir das Geigen beibrachte: Eine Tortur für einen völlig unmusikalischen Menschen.

MÖBIUS. Essen wir nicht weiter?

NEWTON. Der Appetit ist mir vergangen.

EINSTEIN. Schade um das Cordon bleu.

(*Möbius steht auf*)

MÖBIUS. Wir sind drei Physiker.* Die Entscheidung, die wir zu fällen haben, ist eine Entscheidung unter Physikern. Wir müssen wissenschaftlich vorgehen. Wir dürfen uns nicht von Meinungen bestimmen lassen,[1] sondern von logischen Schlüssen. Wir müssen versuchen, das Vernünftige zu finden. Wir dürfen uns keinen Denkfehler leisten, weil ein Fehlschluß zur Katastrophe führen müßte. Der Ausgangspunkt ist klar. Wir haben alle drei das gleiche Ziel im Auge, doch unsere Taktik ist verschieden. Das Ziel ist der Fortgang der Physik. Sie wollen ihr die Freiheit bewahren, Kilton, und streiten ihr die Verantwortung ab.[2] Sie dagegen, Eisler, verpflichten die Physik im Namen der Verantwortung der Machtpolitik eines bestimmten Landes.[3] Wie sieht nun aber die Wirklichkeit aus? Darüber verlange ich Auskunft, soll ich mich entscheiden.

[1] *Wir dürfen uns ... lassen*: we must not let our actions be determined by opinions. (*dürfen* = (1) 'be allowed', (2) 'must', 'ought', especially in sentences such as *Das hätten wir nicht machen dürfen*: We oughtn't to have done that. For *lassen* see note 1, p. 11.)

[2] *streiten ihr ... ab*: deny it any responsibility.

[3] *Sie ... verpflichten die Physik ... Landes*: in the name of responsibility you pledge physics to the power politics of a definite country.

NEWTON. Einige der berühmtesten Physiker erwarten Sie. Besoldung und Unterkunft ideal, die Gegend mörderisch, aber die Klimaanlagen ausgezeichnet.
MÖBIUS. Sind diese Physiker frei?
NEWTON. Mein lieber Möbius. Diese Physiker erklären sich bereit, wissenschaftliche Probleme zu lösen, die für die Landesverteidigung entscheidend sind. Sie müssen daher verstehen —
MÖBIUS. Also nicht frei.

(*Er wendet sich Einstein zu*)

Joseph Eisler. Sie treiben Machtpolitik. Dazu gehört jedoch Macht. Besitzen Sie die?
EINSTEIN. Sie mißverstehen mich, Möbius. Meine Machtpolitik besteht gerade darin, daß ich zu Gunsten einer Partei auf meine Macht verzichtet habe.
MÖBIUS. Können Sie die Partei im Sinne Ihrer Verantwortung lenken oder laufen Sie Gefahr, von der Partei gelenkt zu werden?
EINSTEIN. Möbius! Das ist doch lächerlich. Ich kann natürlich nur hoffen, die Partei befolge meine Ratschläge, mehr nicht. Ohne Hoffnung gibt es nun einmal keine politische Haltung.
MÖBIUS. Sind wenigstens Ihre Physiker frei?
EINSTEIN. Da auch sie für die Landesverteidigung ...
MÖBIUS. Merkwürdig. Jeder preist mir eine andere Theorie an, doch die Realität, die man mir bietet, ist dieselbe: Ein Gefängnis. Da ziehe ich mein Irrenhaus vor. Es gibt mir wenigstens die Sicherheit, von Politikern nicht ausgenützt zu werden.

EINSTEIN. Gewisse Risiken muß man schließlich eingehen.¹

MÖBIUS. Es gibt Risiken, die man nie eingehen darf: Der Untergang der Menschheit ist ein solches. Was die Welt mit den Waffen anrichtet, die sie schon besitzt, wissen wir, was sie mit jenen anrichten würde, die ich ermögliche, können wir uns denken. Dieser Einsicht habe ich mein Handeln untergeordnet.² Ich war arm. Ich besaß eine Frau und drei Kinder. Auf der Universität winkte Ruhm, in der Industrie Geld. Beide Wege waren zu gefährlich. Ich hätte meine Arbeiten veröffentlichen müssen,³ der Umsturz unserer Wissenschaft und das Zusammenbrechen des wirtschaftlichen Gefüges wären die Folgen gewesen. Die Verantwortung zwang mir einen anderen Weg auf. Ich ließ meine akademische Karriere fahren,⁴ die Industrie fallen und überließ meine Familie ihrem Schicksal. Ich wählte die Narrenkappe. Ich gab vor, der König Salomo erscheine mir, und schon sperrte man mich in ein Irrenhaus.

NEWTON. Das war doch keine Lösung!

MÖBIUS. Die Vernunft forderte diesen Schritt. Wir sind in unserer Wissenschaft an die Grenzen des Erkennbaren gestoßen. Wir wissen einige genau erfaßbare Gesetze, einige Grundbeziehungen zwischen un-

---

[1] *Gewisse Risiken muss man schließlich eingehen*: after all one must take certain risks.

[2] *Dieser Einsicht ... untergeordnet*: I have subordinated my actions to this realization.

[3] *Ich hätte ... veröffentlichen müssen*: I ought to have published my works. (See note 2, p. 31.)

[4] *Ich ließ ... fahren*: I abandoned.

begreiflichen Erscheinungen, das ist alles, der gewaltige Rest bleibt Geheimnis, dem Verstande unzugänglich. Wir haben das Ende unseres Weges erreicht. Aber die Menschheit ist noch nicht so weit. Wir haben uns vorgekämpft, nun folgt uns niemand nach, wir sind ins Leere gestoßen.[1] Unsere Wissenschaft ist schrecklich geworden, unsere Forschung gefährlich, unsere Erkenntnisse tödlich. Es gibt für uns Physiker nur noch die Kapitulation vor der Wirklichkeit. Sie ist uns nicht gewachsen.[2] Sie geht an uns zugrunde.[3] Wir müssen unser Wissen zurücknehmen, und ich habe es zurückgenommen. Es gibt keine andere Lösung, auch für euch nicht.

EINSTEIN. Was wollen Sie damit sagen?
MÖBIUS. Ihr müßt bei mir im Irrenhaus bleiben.
NEWTON. Wir?
MÖBIUS. Ihr beide.

(*Schweigen*)

NEWTON. Möbius! Sie können von uns doch nicht verlangen, daß wir ewig —
MÖBIUS. Ihr besitzt Geheimsender?
EINSTEIN. Na und?
MÖBIUS. Ihr benachrichtigt eure Auftraggeber. Ihr hättet euch geirrt. Ich sei wirklich verrückt.
EINSTEIN. Dann sitzen wir hier lebenslänglich.

---

[1] *wir sind ins Leere gestoßen*: we have thrust into the void. (*leer* = empty.)

[2] *Sie ist uns nicht gewachsen*: it (reality) is not equal to us. (There is a note of irony here, as many of Dürrenmatt's characters succumb to reality.)

[3] *Sie geht an uns zugrunde*: it will perish at our hands.

Gescheiterten Spionen kräht kein Hahn mehr nach.¹
MÖBIUS. Meine einzige Chance, doch noch unentdeckt zu bleiben. Nur im Irrenhaus sind wir noch frei. Nur im Irrenhaus dürfen wir noch denken. In der Freiheit sind unsere Gedanken Sprengstoff.
NEWTON. Wir sind doch schließlich nicht verrückt.
MÖBIUS. Aber Mörder.

(*Sie starren ihn verblüfft an*)

NEWTON. Ich protestiere!
EINSTEIN. Das hätten Sie nicht sagen dürfen,² Möbius!
MÖBIUS. Wer tötet, ist ein Mörder, und wir haben getötet. Jeder von uns hatte einen Auftrag, der ihn in diese Anstalt führte. Jeder von uns tötete seine Krankenschwester für einen bestimmten Zweck. Ihr, um eure geheime Mission nicht zu gefährden, ich, weil Schwester Monika an mich glaubte. Sie hielt mich für ein verkanntes Genie. Sie begriff nicht, daß es heute die Pflicht eines Genies ist, verkannt zu bleiben. Töten ist etwas Schreckliches. Ich habe getötet, damit nicht ein noch schrecklicheres Morden anhebe. Nun seid ihr gekommen. Euch kann ich nicht beseitigen, aber vielleicht überzeugen? Sollen unsere Morde sinnlos werden? Entweder haben wir geopfert oder gemordet. Entweder bleiben wir im Irrenhaus oder die Welt wird eines. Entweder löschen wir uns im Gedächtnis der Menschen aus oder

---

¹ *Gescheiterten Spionen ... nach*: nobody bothers about unsuccessful spies.

² *Das hätten Sie nicht sagen dürfen*: you ought not **to have said**, shouldn't have been allowed to say, that.

die Menschheit erlischt.

(*Schweigen*)

NEWTON. Möbius!
MÖBIUS. Kilton?
NEWTON. Diese Anstalt. Diese schrecklichen Pfleger. Diese bucklige Ärztin!
MÖBIUS. Nun?
EINSTEIN. Man sperrt uns ein wie wilde Tiere!
MÖBIUS. Wir sind wilde Tiere. Man darf uns nicht auf die Menschheit loslassen.

(*Schweigen*)

NEWTON. Gibt es wirklich keinen andern Ausweg?
MÖBIUS. Keinen.

(*Schweigen*)

EINSTEIN. Johann Wilhelm Möbius. Ich bin ein anständiger Mensch. Ich bleibe.

(*Schweigen*)

NEWTON. Ich bleibe auch. Für immer.

(*Schweigen*)

MÖBIUS. Ich danke euch. Um der kleinen Chance willen,[2] die nun die Welt doch noch besitzt, davonzukommen.

---

[1] *Entweder löschen wir ... erlischt*: either we erase ourselves from the minds of mankind or humanity becomes extinct. (The weak transitive verb *auslöschen* = to extinguish; the strong intransitive verb *erlöschen* (present, *erlischt*; imperfect, *erlosch*; perfect, *ist erloschen*) = to become extinguished, go out. Notice that *entweder* requires inversion, *oder* does not.)

[2] *Um der kleinen Chance willen*: for the sake of the small chance.

DIE PHYSIKER

(*Er hebt sein Glas*)

Auf unsere Krankenschwestern!*

(*Sie haben sich feierlich erhoben*)

NEWTON. Ich trinke auf Dorothea Moser.
DIE BEIDEN ANDERN. Auf Schwester Dorothea!
NEWTON. Dorothea! Ich mußte dich opfern. Ich gab dir den Tod für deine Liebe! Nun will ich mich deiner würdig erweisen.
EINSTEIN. Ich trinke auf Irene Straub.
DIE BEIDEN ANDERN. Auf Schwester Irene!
EINSTEIN. Irene! Ich mußte dich opfern. Dich zu loben und deine Hingabe zu preisen, will ich vernünftig handeln.
MÖBIUS. Ich trinke auf Monika Stettler.
DIE BEIDEN ANDERN. Auf Schwester Monika!
MÖBIUS. Monika! Ich mußte dich opfern. Deine Liebe segne die Freundschaft, die wir drei Physiker in deinem Namen geschlossen haben. Gib uns die Kraft, als Narren das Geheimnis unserer Wissenschaft treu zu bewahren.

(*Sie trinken, stellen die Gläser auf den Tisch*)

NEWTON. Verwandeln wir uns wieder in Verrückte. Geistern wir als Newton daher.¹
EINSTEIN. Fiedeln wir wieder Kreisler und Beethoven.
MÖBIUS. Lassen wir wieder Salomo erscheinen.
NEWTON. Verrückt, aber weise.
EINSTEIN. Gefangen, aber frei.
MÖBIUS. Physiker, aber unschuldig.

---

¹ *geistern ... daher*: let us haunt the place in the guise of Newton.

(Die drei winken sich zu, gehen auf ihre Zimmer. Der Raum ist leer. Von rechts kommen McArthur und Murillo. Sie tragen nun beide eine schwarze Uniform mit Mütze und Pistolen.* Sie räumen den Tisch ab. McArthur fährt den Wagen mit dem Geschirr nach rechts hinaus, Murillo stellt den runden Tisch vor das Fenster rechts, auf ihn die umgekehrten Stühle, wie beim Aufräumen in einer Wirtschaft. Dann geht auch Murillo nach rechts hinaus. Der Raum ist wieder leer. Dann kommt von rechts Fräulein Doktor Mathilde von Zahnd. Wie immer mit weißem Ärztekittel. Stethoskop. Sie schaut sich um. Endlich kommt noch Sievers, ebenfalls in schwarzer Uniform.)

OBERPFLEGER. Boß.
FRL. DOKTOR. Sievers, das Bild.

(McArthur und Murillo tragen ein großes Porträt in einem schweren goldenen Rahmen herein, einen General darstellend. Sievers hängt das alte Porträt ab und das neue auf)

Der General Leonidas von Zahnd* ist hier besser aufgehoben als bei den Weibern. Er sieht immer noch großartig aus, der alte Haudegen, trotz seines Basedows.[1]* Er liebte Heldentode, und sowas hat in diesem Hause ja nun stattgefunden.

(Sie betrachtet das Bild ihres Vaters)

Dafür kommt der Geheimrat in die Frauenabteilung zu den Millionärinnen. Stellt ihn einstweilen in den Korridor.

(McArthur und Murillo tragen das Bild nach rechts hinaus)

[1] *trotz seines Basedows*: in spite of his goitre. (See note, p. 104.)

Ist Generaldirektor Fröben gekommen mit seinen Helden?

OBERPFLEGER. Sie warten im grünen Salon. Soll ich Sekt und Kaviar bereitstellen?

FRL. DOKTOR. Die Koryphäen* sind nicht da, um zu schlemmen, sondern um zu arbeiten.

(*Sie setzt sich aufs Sofa*)

Holen Sie nun Möbius, Sievers.

OBERPFLEGER. Zu Befehl, Boß.

(*Er geht zu Zimmer Nummer 1, öffnet die Türe*)

Möbius, rauskommen!

(*Möbius erscheint. Wie verklärt*)

MÖBIUS. Eine andächtige Nacht.* Tiefblau und fromm. Die Nacht des mächtigen Königs. Sein weißer Schatten löst sich von der Wand. Seine Augen leuchten.

(*Schweigen*)

FRL. DOKTOR. Möbius. Auf Anordnung des Staatsanwaltes darf ich nur in Anwesenheit eines Wärters mit Ihnen reden.

MÖBIUS. Verstehe, Fräulein Doktor.

FRL. DOKTOR. Was ich zu sagen habe, geht auch Ihre Kollegen an.

(*McArthur und Murillo sind zurückgekommen*)

McArthur and Murillo. Holt die beiden andern.

(*McArthur und Murillo öffnen die Türen Nummer 2 und 3*)

MURILLO UND MCARTHUR. Rauskommen!

(*Newton und Einstein kommen. Auch verklärt*)

NEWTON. Eine geheimnisvolle Nacht. Unendlich und erhaben. Durch das Gitter meines Fensters funkeln Jupiter und Saturn, offenbaren die Gesetze des Alls.

EINSTEIN. Eine glückliche Nacht. Tröstlich und gut. Die Rätsel schweigen, die Fragen sind verstummt. Ich möchte geigen und nie mehr enden.

FRL. DOKTOR. Alec Jasper Kilton und Joseph Eisler, ich habe mit euch[1] zu reden.

(*Die beiden starren sie verwundert an*)

NEWTON. Sie — wissen?

(*Die beiden wollen ihre Revolver ziehen, werden aber von Murillo und McArthur entwaffnet*)

FRL. DOKTOR. Ihr Gespräch, meine Herren, ist abgehört worden; ich hatte schon längst Verdacht geschöpft. Holt Kiltons und Eislers Geheimsender, McArthur und Murillo.

OBERPFLEGER. Die Hände hinter den Nacken, ihr drei!

(*Möbius, Einstein und Newton legen die Hände hinter den Nacken, McArthur und Murillo gehen in Zimmer 2 und 3*)

NEWTON. Drollig!

(*Er lacht. Allein. Gespenstig*)

EINSTEIN. Ich weiß nicht —
NEWTON. Ulkig!

---

[1] *euch*: The change to the familiar plural reflects her hardening attitude.

DIE PHYSIKER

(*Lacht wieder. Verstummt. McArthur und Murillo
kommen mit den Geheimsendern zurück*)

OBERPFLEGER. Hände runter!

(*Die Physiker gehorchen. Schweigen*)

FRL. DOKTOR. Die Scheinwerfer, Sievers.
OBERPFLEGER. OK, Boß.

(*Er hebt die Hand. Von außen tauchen Scheinwerfer
die Physiker in ein blendendes Licht. Gleichzeitig hat
Sievers innen das Licht ausgelöscht.*)

FRL. DOKTOR. Die Villa ist von Wärtern umstellt.[1] Ein Fluchtversuch ist sinnlos.

(*Zu den Pflegern*)

Raus ihr drei!

(*Die drei Pfleger verlassen den Raum, tragen die Waffen
und Geräte hinaus. Schweigen*)

Nur ihr sollt mein Geheimnis wissen. Ihr allein von den Menschen. Weil es keine Rolle mehr spielt,[2] wenn ihr es wißt.

(*Schweigen*)

(*feierlich*) Auch mir ist der goldene König Salomo erschienen.

(*Die drei starren sie verblüfft an*)

MÖBIUS. Salomo?
FRL. DOKTOR. All die Jahre.

(*Newton lacht leise auf*)

---

[1] *von Wärtern umstellt*: surrounded by guards.
[2] *Weil es keine Rolle mehr spielt*: because it is of no further importance.
(Cf. note 1, p. 59.)

(*unbeirrbar*) Zuerst in meinem Arbeitszimmer. An einem Sommerabend. Draußen schien noch die Sonne und im Park hämmerte ein Specht,* als auf einmal der goldene König heranschwebte.¹ Wie ein gewaltiger Engel.

EINSTEIN. Sie ist wahnsinnig geworden.

FRL. DOKTOR. Sein Blick ruhte auf mir. Seine Lippen öffneten sich. Er begann mit seiner Magd zu reden. Er war von den Toten auferstanden, er wollte die Macht wieder übernehmen, die ihm einst hienieden gehörte, er hatte seine Weisheit enthüllt, damit in seinem Namen Möbius auf Erden herrsche.

EINSTEIN. Sie muß interniert werden. Sie gehört in ein Irrenhaus.

FRL. DOKTOR. Aber Möbius verriet ihn. Er versuchte zu verschweigen, was nicht verschwiegen werden konnte. Denn was ihm offenbart worden war, ist kein Geheimnis. Weil es denkbar ist. Alles Denkbare wird einmal gedacht.* Jetzt oder in der Zukunft. Was Salomo gefunden hatte, kann einmal auch ein anderer finden, es sollte die Tat des goldenen Königs bleiben, das Mittel zu seiner heiligen Weltherrschaft und so suchte er mich auf, seine unwürdige Dienerin.

EINSTEIN (*eindringlich*). Sie sind verrückt. Hören Sie, Sie sind verrückt.

FRL. DOKTOR. Er befahl mir, Möbius abzusetzen und an seiner Stelle zu herrschen. Ich gehorchte dem Befehl. Ich war Ärztin und Möbius mein Patient. Ich konnte mit ihm tun, was ich wollte. Ich betäubte ihn, jahrelang, immer wieder, und photokopierte die Aufzeichnungen des goldenen Königs, bis ich auch

¹ *heranschwebte*: came towards me in hovering flight.

die letzten Seiten besaß.

NEWTON. Sie sind übergeschnappt! Vollkommen! Begreifen Sie doch endlich! (*leise*) Wir alle sind übergeschnappt.

FRL. DOKTOR. Ich ging behutsam vor. Ich beutete zuerst nur wenige Erfindungen aus, das nötige Kapital anzusammeln. Dann gründete ich Riesenwerke, erstand eine Fabrik um die andere[1] und baute einen mächtigen Trust auf. Ich werde das System aller möglichen Erfindungen auswerten, meine Herren.

MÖBIUS (*eindringlich*). Fräulein Doktor Mathilde von Zahnd: Sie sind krank. Salomo ist nicht wirklich. Er ist mir nie erschienen.

FRL. DOKTOR. Sie lügen.

MÖBIUS. Ich habe ihn nur erfunden, um meine Entdeckungen geheim zu halten.

FRL. DOKTOR. Sie verleugnen ihn.

MÖBIUS. Nehmen Sie Vernunft an. Sehen Sie doch ein, daß Sie verrückt sind.*

FRL. DOKTOR. Ebensowenig wie Sie.

MÖBIUS. Dann muß ich der Welt die Wahrheit entgegenschreien. Sie beuteten mich all die Jahre aus. Schamlos. Sogar meine arme Frau ließen Sie noch zahlen.

FRL. DOKTOR. Sie sind machtlos, Möbius. Auch wenn Ihre Stimme in die Welt hinausdränge, würde man Ihnen nicht glauben. Denn für die Öffentlichkeit sind Sie nichts anderes als ein gefährlicher Verrückter. Durch Ihren Mord.[2]

---

[1] *erstand ... um die andere*: bought one factory after the other.
[2] *Durch Ihren Mord*: Cf. note 3, p. 27.

(*Die drei ahnen die Wahrheit*)*

MÖBIUS. Monika?
EINSTEIN. Irene?
NEWTON. Dorothea?
FRL. DOKTOR. Ich nahm nur eine Gelegenheit wahr. Das Wissen Salomos mußte gesichert und euer Verrat bestraft werden. Ich mußte euch unschädlich machen. Durch eure Morde. Ich hetzte die drei Krankenschwestern auf euch.*[1] Mit eurem Handeln konnte ich rechnen. Ihr waret bestimmbar wie Automaten und habt getötet wie Henker.

(*Möbius will sich auf sie stürzen, Einstein hält ihn zurück*)

Es ist sinnlos, Möbius, sich auf mich zu stürzen. So wie es sinnlos war, Manuskripte zu verbrennen, die ich schon besaß.

(*Möbius wendet sich ab*)

Was euch umgibt, sind nicht mehr die Mauern einer Anstalt. Dieses Haus ist die Schatzkammer meines Trusts. Es umschließt drei Physiker, die allein außer mir die Wahrheit wissen. Was euch in Bann hält,[2] sind keine Irrenwärter: Sievers ist der Chef meiner Werkpolizei. Ihr seid in euer eigenes Gefängnis geflüchtet.[3] Salomo hat durch euch gedacht, durch euch gehandelt, und nun vernichtet er euch. Durch mich.

---

[1] *Ich hetzte die drei Krankenschwester auf euch*: I incited the three nurses to go after you.

[2] *in Bann hält*: keeps you under constraint.

[3] *Ihr seid in euer eigenes Gefängnis geflüchtet*: you have taken refuge in your own prison. (This is the **extremely** paradoxical **situation** on which the play is built up.)

(*Schweigen*)

Ich aber übernehme seine Macht. Ich fürchte mich nicht. Meine Anstalt ist voll von verrückten Verwandten, mit Schmuck behängt und Orden.¹* Ich bin die letzte Normale meiner Familie. Das Ende. Unfruchtbar, nur noch zur Nächstenliebe geeignet. Da erbarmte sich Salomo meiner.² Er, der tausend Weiber besitzt, wählte mich aus. Nun werde ich mächtiger sein als meine Väter.³ Mein Trust wird herrschen, die Länder, die Kontinente erobern, das Sonnensystem ausbeuten, nach dem Andromedanebel* fahren. Die Rechnung ist aufgegangen.⁴ Nicht zu Gunsten der Welt, aber zu Gunsten einer alten, buckligen Jungfrau.

(*Sie läutet mit einer kleinen Glocke. Von rechts kommt der Oberpfleger*)

OBERPFLEGER. Boß?
FRL. DOKTOR. Gehen wir, Sievers. Der Verwaltungsrat wartet. Das Weltunternehmen startet, die Produktion rollt an.

---

¹ *mit Schmuck behängt und Orden*: covered with decorations and orders. (See note, p. 106.)
² *erbarmte sich Salomo meiner*: Solomon took pity on me. (*erbarmen* + genitive; *meiner* is the genitive of *ich*.)
³ *mächtiger sein als meine Väter*: more powerful than my fathers. (It is fairly common usage to add short phrases, especially with *als* = than, to an infinitive or past participle.)
⁴ *Die Rechnung ist aufgegangen*: the sum has worked out (i.e. without a remainder). (Translate: 'It has all worked out nicely.) Cf. Rilke's Fifth Elegy, *Les Saltimbanques*: 'Wo die vielstellige Rechnung zahlenlos aufgeht': 'where the many-digited sum works out to zero'.

(*Sie geht mit dem Oberpfleger nach rechts hinaus. Die drei Physiker sind allein. Stille. Alles ist ausgespielt. Schweigen.*)

NEWTON. Es ist aus.

(*Er setzt sich aufs Sofa*)

EINSTEIN. Die Welt ist in die Hände einer verrückten Irrenärztin gefallen.

(*Er setzt sich zu Newton*)

MÖBIUS. Was einmal gedacht wurde, kann nicht mehr zurückgenommen werden.

(*Möbius setzt sich auf den Sessel links vom Sofa. Schweigen. Sie starren vor sich hin. Dann reden sie ganz ruhig, selbstverständlich, stellen sich einfach dem Publikum vor.*)*

NEWTON. Ich bin Newton. Sir Isaak Newton. Geboren am 4. Januar 1643 in Woolsthorpe bei Grantham. Ich bin Präsident der Royal-Society.* Aber es braucht sich deshalb keiner zu erheben. Ich schrieb: Die mathematischen Grundlagen der Naturwissenschaft. Ich sagte: Hypotheses non fingo.[1] In der experimentellen Optik, in der theoretischen Mechanik und in der höheren Mathematik sind meine Leistungen nicht unwichtig, aber die Frage nach dem Wesen der Schwerkraft mußte ich offen lassen. Ich schrieb auch theologische Bücher. Bemerkungen zum Propheten Daniel und zur Johannes-Apokalypse.* Ich bin Newton. Sir Isaak Newton. Ich bin Präsident der Royal-Society.

(*Er erhebt sich und geht auf sein Zimmer*)

[1] *Hypotheses non fingo*: 'I don't make hypotheses'.

DIE PHYSIKER

EINSTEIN. Ich bin Einstein. Professor Albert Einstein. Geboren am 14. März 1879 in Ulm. 1902 wurde ich Experte am eidgenössischen Patentamt in Bern. Dort stellte ich meine spezielle Relativitätstheorie auf, die die Physik veränderte. Dann wurde ich Mitglied der Preußischen Akademie der Wissenschaft. Später wurde ich Emigrant. Weil ich ein Jude bin. Von mir stammt die Formel $E = mc^2$,* der Schlüssel zur Umwandlung von Materie in Energie. Ich liebe die Menschen und liebe meine Geige, aber auf meine Empfehlung hin baute man die Atombombe. Ich bin Einstein. Professor Albert Einstein. Geboren am 14. März 1879 in Ulm.

(*Er erhebt sich und geht in sein Zimmer. Dann hört man ihn geigen. Kreisler. Liebesleid.*)

MÖBIUS. Ich bin Salomo. Ich bin der arme König Salomo. Einst war ich unermeßlich reich, weise und gottesfürchtig. Ob meiner Macht[1] erzitterten die Gewaltigen. Ich war ein Fürst des Friedens und der Gerechtigkeit. Aber meine Weisheit zerstörte meine Gottesfurcht, und als ich Gott nicht mehr fürchtete, zerstörte meine Weisheit meinen Reichtum. Nun sind die Städte tot, über die ich regierte, mein Reich leer, das mir anvertraut worden war, eine blauschimmernde Wüste, und, irgendwo, um einen kleinen, gelben, namenlosen[2] Stern, kreist, sinnlos,[3] immerzu,

---

[1] *Ob meiner Macht*: on account of my power. (*Ob* + genitive = on account of.)

[2] *namenlos*: nameless. (Because no one will be left to name it.)

[3] *sinnlos*: senselessly. (Because there will be no life on it. The collapse of Solomon's empire symbolises the final destruction of the earth: this is the grim warning of the play as a whole.)

die radioaktive Erde. Ich bin Salomo, ich bin Salomo, ich bin der arme König Salomo.

(*Er geht auf sein Zimmer. Nun ist der Salon leer. Nur noch die Geige Einsteins ist zu hören.*)

ENDE

21 PUNKTE ZU DEN PHYSIKERN

1. *Ich gehe nicht von einer These, sondern von einer Geschichte aus.*

2. *Geht man von einer Geschichte aus, muß sie zu Ende gedacht werden.*

3. *Eine Geschichte ist dann zu Ende gedacht, wenn sie ihre schlimmstmögliche Wendung genommen hat.*

4. *Die schlimmst-mögliche Wendung ist nicht voraussehbar. Sie tritt durch Zufall[1] ein.*

5. *Die Kunst des Dramatikers besteht darin, in einer Handlung den Zufall möglichst wirksam einzusetzen.[2]*

6. *Träger einer dramatischen Handlung sind Menschen.*

7. *Der Zufall in einer dramatischen Handlung besteht darin, wann und wo wer zufällig wem begegnet.[3]*

---

[1] *Zufall*: chance. (This is in Dürrenmatt another name for reality, the irrational basis of life on earth.)

[2] *besteht darin, in einer Handlung den Zufall möglichst wirksam einzusetzen*: consists in making the most effective use of chance.

[3] *wann und wo wer zufällig wem begegnet*: when and where someone accidentally meets someone else.

8. *Je planmäßiger die Menschen vorgehen, desto wirksamer vermag sie der Zufall zu treffen.*[1]

9. *Planmäßig vorgehende Menschen wollen ein bestimmtes Ziel erreichen. Der Zufall trifft sie dann am schlimmsten, wenn sie durch ihn das Gegenteil ihres Ziels erreichen: Das, was sie befürchteten, was sie zu vermeiden suchten (z. B. Oedipus).*

10. *Eine solche Geschichte ist zwar grotesk, aber nicht absurd (sinnwidrig).*

11. *Sie ist paradox.**

12. *Ebensowenig wie die Logiker können die Dramatiker das Paradoxe vermeiden.*

13. *Ebensowenig wie die Logiker können die Physiker das Paradoxe vermeiden.*

14. *Ein Drama über die Physiker muß paradox sein.*

15. *Es kann nicht den Inhalt der Physik zum Ziele haben, sondern nur ihre Auswirkung.*

16. *Der Inhalt der Physik geht die Physiker an,*[2] *die Auswirkung alle Menschen.*

17. *Was alle angeht, können nur alle lösen.**

---

[1] *Je planmäßiger die Menschen ... zu treffen*: the more planning people put into their efforts, the more effectively can chance strike them.

[2] *Der Inhalt der Physik geht die Physiker an*: the content of physics concerns the physicists.

18. *Jeder Versuch eines Einzelnen, für sich zu lösen, was alle angeht, muß scheitern.**

19. *Im Paradoxen erscheint die Wirklichkeit.*

20. *Wer dem Paradoxen gegenübersteht, setzt sich der Wirklichkeit aus.*

21. *Die Dramatik kann den Zuschauer überlisten, sich der Wirklichkeit auszusetzen, aber nicht zwingen, ihr standzuhalten oder sie gar zu bewältigen.*

BIBLIOGRAPHY

(a) *Works by Dürrenmatt*

(Published by Verlag der Arche, Zürich, except where otherwise stated.)

PLAYS

Es steht geschrieben (1947)
Der Blinde (1948)
Romulus der Große (1949; revised 1957)
Die Ehe des Herrn Mississipi (1952)
Ein Engel kommt nach Babylon (1953)
Der Besuch der alten Dame (1956)
Frank V (1959)
Die Physiker (1962)
Herkules und der Stall des Augias (1963)
Der Meteor (1966)

RADIO PLAYS

Der Doppelgänger (1946)
Der Prozeß um des Esels Schatten (1951; published 1958)
Nächtliches Gespräch (1952; published 1957)
Stranitzky und der Nationalheld (1953)
Herkules und der Stall des Augias (1954)
Das Unternehmen der Wega (1955)
Abendstunde im Spätherbst (1957)

NOVELS AND STORIES

Die Stadt (1952)
Der Richter und sein Henker (1952)
Der Verdacht (1953)
Grieche sucht Griechin (1955)
Die Panne (1956)
Das Versprechen (1958)

ESSAYS, SPEECHES

Theaterprobleme (1955)
Friedrich Schiller: Eine Rede (1960)
Der Rest ist Dank: Eine Rede (1961)

Die Heimat im Plakat. Ein Buch für Schweizer Kinder, Diogenes Verlag, Zürich, 1964. (Mainly sketches with slogans criticizing aspects of Swiss life.)

(b) Books on Dürrenmatt

H. Bänziger, *Frisch und Dürrenmatt*, Francke Verlag, Bern, 1960.

Elisabeth Brock-Sulzer, *Friedrich Dürrenmatt: Stationen seines Werkes*, Verlag der Arche, Zürich, 1960; rev. ed., 1964.

Therese Poser, 'Friedrich Dürrenmatt', in *Zur Interpretation des Modernen Dramas* (ed. R. Geißler), Verlag Moritz Diesterweg, Frankfurt a.M., 1959.

Editor's Note: It was considered advisable to give a fairly detailed critical summary of Dürrenmatt's main plays rather than a superficial criticism of all his works. For this reason no attempt has been made to assess his other prose writings and radio plays.

NOTES

1 **Ort:** Dürrenmatt takes great pains in the stage directions to give as complete a background as possible to the setting for the action. The country where the villa is located is not given, though most of the descriptions suggest the lakeside region near Dürrenmatt's home at Neuchâtel, and the reference to the Tobler chocolate factory (p. 27) also indicates a Swiss setting. It is not Dürrenmatt's intention, however, to stress any particular country, the implication being that the events to be enacted are the concern of humanity as a whole. The prison which the villa ultimately becomes is anticipated by the groups of prisoners digging in the vicinity; this is in keeping with the classical structure of the play, with its many large and small closely interlocking parts. The stage directions also tell of the first murder and describe in detail the second, which has just occurred. This use of the so-called analytical method enables Dürrenmatt to streamline the action and focus the attention of the spectators on the essentials of the play.

2 **die Einheit von Raum, Zeit und Handlung:** 'the unities of place, time, and action', observed in the Greek classical drama and discussed at some length by Aristotle; they demanded a concise, unified action with no sub-plots, lasting no longer than twenty-four hours and taking place in the same location, often a single room.

2 **C. G. Jung**: Carl Gustav Jung (1875–1961), the well-known Swiss psychologist and one-time associate of Freud.

2 **Ernis Glasmalereien**: 'Erni's stained-glass windows'. Hans Erni (b. 1909) is a well-known Swiss painter and sculptor.

4 **Beethoven**: Ludwig van Beethoven (1770–1827), the great German composer.

4 **Kreutzersonate**: 'Kreutzer Sonata', the popular name of Beethoven's violin and pianoforte Sonata in A major, Opus 47. Beethoven first played it in public with the mulatto violinist George Bridgetower, who would have been the dedicatee but for a quarrel between the two. It was then dedicated to the French violinist Rodolfe Kreutzer (1766–1831), the son of German parents who settled in Versailles.

4 **Kassettendecke**: an ornate ceiling, having a recessed circle in the centre, flanked by recessed rectangles and other plaster-work decorations.

4 **Satyrspiel**: 'satyr play'. This is a play, peculiar to the ancient Greeks, in which satyrs formed the chorus. Being half-human, half-animal, they set the tone of the play by their wild excesses and unrestrained merriment. As the Greek tragedy developed, it became the custom to perform such a play as a light relief after a tragedy, especially after a trilogy. Here Dürrenmatt gives the light relief first and reserves the tragedy for the end of the action.

5 **Einstein**: Albert Einstein (1879–1955), the outstanding physicist of modern times. He was born in Ulm, Württemberg; at the age of fifteen he went to Switzerland, where from 1902 he worked in the Patents

Office in Berne. After being Professor of Physics at Zürich and Prague he took charge of the Kaiser-Wilhelm Institute for Physics in Berlin from the year 1914. In 1934 the Hitler régime forced him to emigrate to the U.S.A. In his general and special relativity theories he widened and extended the work of Newton and explained some of the discrepancies. He made further valuable contributions to science by his extension of Planck's quantum theory. See also the notes on *die einheitliche Feldtheorie* (p. 103) and $E = mc^2$ (p. 106).

6 **Newton**: Sir Isaac Newton (1643–1727), son of a farmer, went to Trinity College, Cambridge, in 1660, and was Professor of Physics there from 1669 to 1701. In 1703 he became President of the Royal Society. He was a celebrated physicist, mathematician, and astronomer, whose discoveries lie at the basis of modern science. He proved that the force of gravity attracting two bodies to each other was proportional to the product of their masses divided by the square of the distance between them. With this discovery he could forecast the orbits of the planets.

16 **Brahmssonate**: Johannes Brahms (1833–97) was a very versatile German composer. His main interest was in chamber music.

21 **Möbius**: The choice of this name is probably a tribute to the German astronomer and mathematician, August Ferdinand Möbius (1790–1868), who became Professor of Astronomy at Leipzig University and director of the observatory. His main work, *Der baryzentrische Kalkül*, deals with the properties of the mean point or centre of mass and abounds in suggestions and foreshadowings of some of the most striking dis-

coveries of recent times, such, for example, as are found in Sir William R. Hamilton's *Quaternions*. Möbius is best remembered by the 'Möbiusfläche' or 'Möbius strip', which was a rectangular strip, stuck together to form a ring by fixing the underside of one edge to the upper side of the other. This twisted ring had many peculiar, even paradoxical, qualities: for example, if one starts cutting it down the middle, one would expect to finish up with two separate rings; instead only one large ring remains. The name is therefore appropriate for the central figure in a play full of twists and paradoxes. Whether this is intentional or not is a matter for speculation.

25 **auf den Marianen**: 'on the Marianas'. These islands in the Pacific Ocean are to the east of the Philippines and about half-way between New Guinea and Japan. From 1899 to 1919 they were a German colony.

25 **Salomo**: Solomon, younger son of David and Bathsheba; the latter succeeded in persuading David to name him king in preference to his elder brother Adonijah. He was able to maintain the powerful position of his kingdom, as related in the first Book of Kings. The period of his rule was later looked upon as a golden age and his wisdom became proverbial. Many of the more recent books of the Old Testament, e.g. the Proverbs and the Psalms, were attributed to him. In the traditions of the Orient, Solomon became the ideal of a wise and mighty ruler; later it was said that he had powers over the realm of ghosts and devils. He is therefore an appropriate choice for the apparition which makes periodic visits to Möbius with revelations concerning the secrets of nature.

DIE PHYSIKER

34 **Buxtehude**: Dietrich Buxtehude (1637–1707) was a Swedish organist at the Marienkirche in Lübeck, where his playing was widely acclaimed, especially after the *Abendmusiken* (1673). Bach made a pilgrimage on foot from Arnstadt to Lübeck in order to learn from this master and composer of organ music.

34 **Inniger, Buben, inniger**: *inniger* = 'more fervently' or 'with more feeling'. A similar, rather ridiculous situation occurs in *Der Besuch der alten Dame*, where one of the heroine's many husbands is told to 'ponder deeply'.

34 **des Hohen Liedes**: *Das Hohe Lied*, the Song of Songs (or Song of Solomon), contains some of the most beautiful lyrical passages of the Old Testament.

34 **Sulamith ... die Rehzwillinge**: cf. Song of Songs 6: 13 and 7: 3. Shulamite is the bride.

35 **Wir hauten ins Weltall ab**: 'We pushed off into the universe'. This 'psalm' of the astronauts is intended to convince Möbius's wife of his insanity and to make the parting easier. The contrast between the 'breathing earth' and the dead stars indicates the fate in store for this world if the physicists' inventions are misused. This theme is also taken up at the end of the play (cf. pp. 87–88). The general tone of the song is critical of ventures into space at a time when there is so much to be done on an earth full of beauty and wonder. Dürrenmatt is lavish in his praise of the earth. (Cf. *Ein Engel kommt nach Babylon, Das Unternehmen der Wega*.)

37 **Marianengraben**: 'Marianas Trench', the name given to a crescent-shaped hollow in the sea-bed, lying a little to the east of the islands, about 1,400 miles long and 36,198 feet deep at its southern end.

39 **das System aller möglichen Erfindungen**: 'the

system of all possible inventions' (cf. note, p. 103). A successful solution explaining a unified field theory would give the answer to all questions in science and technology.

43 **Auch Schwester Irene und ich liebten uns**: This speech, anticipating the next murder, is another example of the contrapuntal effect, the interlacing of motives, actions, and speeches, which is typical of the play and an essential part of its classical structure.

49 **Vor Glück**: 'of (through) happiness'. Notice how this remark and the romantic situation contrast sharply with the ensuing murder, which in its turn contrasts with Newton's indifferent reaction to the news. This sudden reversal of fate — the building-up of an atmosphere and its abrupt destruction through the seemingly irrational forces of reality — anticipates and underlines the central theme, which reaches its climax in the complete and utter discomfiture of the last act.

49 **Kreisler**: Fritz Kreisler (1875–1962), the celebrated Viennese violinist and composer, who settled in America in 1915.

49 **Rosmarin**: 'rosemary', a fragrant evergreen shrub with blue flowers, used as a token of remembrance, especially at funerals; hence the appropriateness of this particular piece of music.

ACT II

50 **du kannst jetzt photographieren ... Wie hieß die Schwester?**: Notice the almost word-for-word repetition of the opening act. Apart from being humorous, this recapitulation of previous scenes or speeches is a further element in the close-knit classical structure of the play. Cf. notes on *Auch Schwester Irene*

und ich liebten uns (p. 43) and *Auf unsere Krankenschwestern!* (p. 77).

51 **den Mörder**: This time the Fräulein Doktor is corrected for using the word 'murderer'.

51 **Dieser dritte Unglücksfall ...**: Notice the short sentences of almost equal length: this fits in well with the short crisp sentences or phrases which make up the bulk of the dialogue. This regular division of speeches or dialogues is well adapted to the larger but none the less very symmetrical dividing-up of the play as a whole.

52 **zwei riesenhafte Pfleger**: Dürrenmatt rarely neglects an opportunity to introduce an incongruous note. Apart from the stark difference between the burly warders and the refinement of the meal — Dresden china, silver cutlery, etc. — the ex-boxers would seem to represent that brute force and ruthlessness which so often has the last word in decisions made by human beings in the 'Wurstelei unseres Jahrhunderts'. Sievers and his helpers have their counterparts in the ex-gangsters who assist the rich old lady Claire in *Der Besuch der alten Dame*.

52 **Das Meißnerporzellan**: 'Dresden china'; this has been manufactured, first in Dresden, then in the neighbouring town of Meißen, since 1710, following on the success of experiments made on behalf of Augustus II ('August der Starke'), Elector of Saxony, by Johann Friedrich Böttger, who founded the first factory. The elegance and artistic merit of Dresden china figures soon brought universal acclaim. The identifying mark is a pair of crossed swords.

54 **Liebesleid**: 'Love's Sorrow'; the music is again appropriate to the situation.

59 **Entsprechungslehre**: A reference to the Danish Nobel Prize winner for physics, Niels Bohr (1885–1962), whose *Korrespondenzprinzip* and other writings sought to show the connection between quantum and atomic physics.

60 **verstehe**: for *Ich verstehe*. Note how this dialogue is repeated a few minutes later by Möbius and Einstein (cf. note to *Auch Schwester Irene und ich liebten uns*, p. 43). By the repetition of these speeches and the similarity of other speeches at the close of the act, the scientists seem to acquire a puppet-like quality. This also fits in well with the sentiment expressed: the individual lack of responsibility for crimes perpetrated on higher authority, a plea often put forward at the Nuremberg Trials.

60 **Bach**: Johann Sebastian Bach (1685–1750), the great German composer, many of whose works were based on Biblical themes.

62 **Der Entdecker des Eisler-Effekts?**: 'The discoverer of the Eisler effect?' An indirect allusion to the Doppler effect, named after the Austrian scientist Christian Johann Doppler (1803–53); this explained why a source of sound, e.g. a train whistle, apparently increases in pitch on approaching a stationary observer and thereafter seems to decrease.

63 **Henkersmahlzeit**: 'hangman's meal', meal given to a prisoner before execution. Dürrenmatt's love of contrast causes him often to use a good meal as the preamble to the complete discomfiture or death of one of the participants (cf. Introduction, p. lxiii).

64 **Patient Beutler!**: The change in nomenclature contrasts with the earlier scene where the guards laid the table for 'die lieben Kranken'.

66 **Nobelpreis**: 'Nobel Prize', named after Alfred Nobel, the Swedish chemist and industrialist, born 1833 in Stockholm, died 1896 in San Remo. He gained world renown and an enormous fortune from his invention of dynamite in the early 1860s. By 1875 he had interests in fifteen dynamite factories in leading industrial countries. He never married and left most of his fortune — about 32 million Swedish crowns — to form the Nobel Foundation, a trust fund from which are made annually five awards running into several thousands of pounds. The first three prizes are given for the best achievements in physics, chemistry, and medicine or physiology; the fourth is for the best literary work and the fifth, paradoxically, for the best contribution to the promotion of peace and brotherhood on earth. The very high value of the prizes and the fact that no account is taken of nationality or race has given the awards a unique standing in the cultural life of the twentieth century. The gaining of a Nobel Prize is undoubtedly one of the highest honours in the field of science or literature.

67 **die einheitliche Feldtheorie**: Einstein worked out separate mathematical equations explaining the working of the three main forces with which physics is concerned, i.e. gravity, magnetism, and electricity. It was felt that there ought to be some general law or theory which would explain the workings of all three and show a common bond between them. Moreover, such a unified theory of relativity, or unified field theory, might be able to explain the working of nuclear forces and especially the behaviour of elementary particles which make up the atom. Hence the reference to 'Elementarteilchen'.

Einstein's researches after 1917 were mainly devoted to solving the problem of the unified theory of relativity.

69 **ein jämmerlicher Ästhet**: 'a wretched aesthete', i.e. a person professing a special or even exaggerated opinion of the beautiful. This is in answer to Kilton's insistence on freedom for the scientist, with the implication that he is interested in science for its own sake and little concerned about the uses to which it is put, or the powers which control it.

71 **Wir sind drei Physiker**: In this and subsequent speeches Möbius places the responsibility for their inventions squarely on the shoulders of the scientists. This does not mean, in Dürrenmatt's view, that other people have no responsibility.

77 **Auf unsere Krankenschwestern!**: The balanced structure of this dialogue and also of the speeches made by the three physicists at the end of the play are further examples of the care taken by Dürrenmatt to give the play the required classical polish. They bear some resemblance to the chorus in classical Greek drama.

78 **eine schwarze Uniform mit Mütze und Pistolen**: Notice the contrast between the exalted mood of the physicists and the sudden, ominous appearance of the guards. (Cf. Möbius's exalted mood prior to the murder.) The change of atmosphere becomes even more marked with the order 'Rauskommen!' a few moments later.

78 **Der General Leonidas von Zahnd**: Cf. the Fräulein Doktor's speech on p. 17. The change in the portraits is in keeping with her changed attitude.

78 **Basedow** (m.), 'goitre': Otherwise called *die Base-*

dowsche Krankheit, after the German doctor Karl von Basedow (1799–1854) who first described it in 1840. Main symptoms are swelling of the thyroid gland in the neck and protruding eyes; it is also known as Graves' disease, after the English doctor who investigated it in 1844.

79 **Die Koryphäen**: From the Greek word for 'summit'; they were the chorus-leaders in the ancient Greek drama. Later the term came to be applied to any leaders in art or science.

79 **Eine andächtige Nacht**: See note to *Auf unsere Krankenschwestern!*, p. 104.

82 **ein Specht**: The woodpecker also forms part of the setting for a romantic scene in *Der Besuch der alten Dame*.

82 **Alles Denkbare wird einmal gedacht**: A significant utterance, which seems to go beyond the immediate context. The first implication is that no individual, however talented, can hope to have a monopoly of some branch of knowledge; the second is that no individual is capable of solving, by himself, problems that affect all mankind; thirdly, that Möbius should not evade the responsibility for controlling his knowledge.

83 **Sehen Sie doch ein, daß Sie verrückt sind**: 'Do realize that you are mad.' Dürrenmatt is a past master in extracting comedy from desperate situations.

84 **ahnen die Wahrheit**: 'suspect the truth'. The paradox on which the play is based reaches here its culminating point: the murders, most unwillingly committed with a single aim in view, have not only been planned and foreseen by the Fräulein Doktor, but also give her complete power over the scientists, who have thus by their own sacrifices brought about the very

thing they were striving to avoid. Cf. No. 9 of the '21 Punkte', p. 90.

84 **ich hetzte ... auf euch:** This is probably the weakest link in the plot, another perhaps being when Einstein and Newton elect to stay behind with Möbius even though they do not know his secret. In any case Dürrenmatt's first interest was never the 'naturalness' of his characters, who are rarely psychologically convincing.

85 **mit Schmuck behängt und Orden:** In a crazy world such as ours, honours and wealth are heaped on those who least deserve them. Dürrenmatt rarely omits an opportunity to ridicule the actions of political, military, and other leaders who are largely responsible for the chaotic state of affairs on this beautiful earth.

85 **Andromedanebel:** The Andromeda nebula, a cluster of stars in the northern heavens.

86 **stellen sich einfach dem Publikum vor:** 'Entstofflichung' or disillusionment of the theatre is discussed in the Introduction, pp. xi, xii, xxi.

86 **Royal-Society:** founded in 1660 to further the study of science and mathematics.

86 **Johannes-Apokalypse:** the Revelation of St. John the Divine, the last book of the New Testament.

87 $E = mc^2$: In this often-quoted equation E stands for rest mass energy, m for mass, and c for the velocity of light, which is constant at 186,000 miles per second. The basic implication is that an increase in energy causes an increase in mass; but because c^2 is so large, an enormous increase in energy will only produce a very small increase in mass. The reverse applies when the atom is split; a very small change in mass releases an

DIE PHYSIKER

enormous amount of energy. Hence the reference to this formula as the key to the changing of mass into energy and Einstein's claim to responsibility for the atom bomb.

21 PUNKTE ZU DEN PHYSIKERN

90 **paradox:** A paradox is defined as follows: a statement, view, or doctrine contrary to received opinion; an assertion, seemingly absurd, but really correct; a self-contradictory or essentially false or absurd statement; a person, thing, or phenomenon at variance with normal ideas of what is probable, natural, or possible. The normal view here would be that the physicists' efforts would be crowned with at least some measure of success; instead, their very efforts lead them to their doom.

90–91 **Punkte 17 and 18:** These are Dürrenmatt's most cherished convictions: the sense of responsibility of the ordinary individual is more likely to result in a solution of our problems than if these are left to the so-called 'great' individuals, who are in any case bound to fall a prey to 'Zufall' or 'Wirklichkeit'. (Cf. note on *mit Schmuck behängt und Orden*, p. 85.)

VOCABULARY

All words are given, with the exception of a few very common words. Separable prefixes are followed by a hyphen. Parts of strong verbs only are given in full

ab-danken, resign, abdicate, give up
das Abendbrot(-e), supper
das Abendland, Western world, Occident
abends, in the evening
ab-gehen (-ging, -gegangen; sein), go off, depart
die Abgeschlossenheit, isolation confinement
der Abgrund(ⁿe), pit, abyss
die Abhandlung(-en), treatise, dissertation
ab-hängen, to take down (picture)
ab-hauen (-hieb, -gehauen), scram, clear off
sich ab-heben (-hob, -gehoben) von, contrast with, stand out against
ab-hören, eavesdrop, listen in to, tap (message)
das Abitur(-e), final school-leaving examination; 'A'-level examination
ab-lehnen, refuse, turn down
sich ab-mühen, exert oneself, struggle
ab-nehmen (-nahm, -genommen), take off, decrease
ab-räumen, remove, clear away
die Abreise(-n), departure

ab-schieben (-schob, -geschoben), push off, go
der Abschied(-e), leave-taking, farewell, departure
ab-schließen (-schloß, -geschlossen), lock, close; conclude
abseits, away from
ab-setzen, depose
die Absicht(-en), intention, design
sich ab-spielen, take place, happen
ab-streiten (-stritt, -gestritten), dispute, deny
die Abteilung(-en), section, department, ward
ab-treiben (-trieb, -getrieben; sein, intrans.), drive off, off one's course, drift off
ab-wenden (-wandte, -gewandt, or weak), turn away from
ab-wischen, wipe away
ab-zirkeln, define sharply
ahnen, suspect, have a foreboding of
das All, universe
allein, alone, only
die Alleinerbin(-nen), sole inheritress
das Allgemeingut, common property
allmählich, gradually
alt, old; der Älteste, the eldest (boy)

das **Alter**, age
der **Altersunterschied**(*–e*), difference in age
die **Altstadt**(*⸗e*), old part of the town
  an-beißen (*-biß, -gebissen*), bite at, off
  andächtig, pious devout, serene
das **Andante**(*–s*), andante; movement in moderately slow time (Ital.)
  ändern, alter, change
  anders als, different from, other than
der **Andromedanebel**, Andromeda nebula
die **Anerkennung**(*–en*), recognition
der **Anfall**(*⸗e*), attack, fit
der **Anfänger**(*–*), beginner
  anfänglich, in the beginning, at first
  an-flehen, implore, beseech
die **Anforderung**(*–en*), requirement, demand
  an-geben (*-gab, -gegeben*), state, assert
  angeblich, allegedly
  angegriffen, affected, attacked
  an-gehen (*-ging, -gegangen*), concern; (*sein*) begin
der **Angehörige** (adj. noun), relative
die **Angelegenheit**(*–en*), affair, matter
  angenehm, pleasant
das **Angesicht**(*–er*), face, countenance
  angreifen (*-griff, -gegriffen*), attack
der **Angriff**(*–e*), attack; *in — nehmen* (*nahm, genommen*), set about
  an-heben (*-hob, -gehoben*), begin
  an-läuten, ring up
  an-nehmen (*-nahm, -genommen*), assume, accept
  an-ordnen, order, command
die **Anordnung** (*–en*), order, instruction, arrangement
  an-preisen (*-pries, -gepriesen*), extol, praise
das **Anraten**, advice; *auf — von* (or+gen.), on the advice of
  an-richten, prepare, set out; produce, cause
  an-rollen (*sein*, intrans.), roll on, forwards; get going
  an-sammeln, accumulate, collect
  an-schauen, look at
  anscheinend, seemingly, apparently
  an-schreien (*-schrie, -geschrien*), scream at, shout at
die **Ansicht**(*–en*), view, opinion
  an-sprechen (*-sprach, -gesprochen*), speak to, address
  anspruchslos, unassuming
die **Anstalt**(*–en*), institution
  anständig, decent, respectable
  an-starren, stare at
  anstelle von, instead of
  an-stellen, employ, engage
  anstößig, objectionable
  an-strengen, exert, strain; be strenuous, exhaust
  an-treten (*-trat, -getreten*), begin (journey, etc.)
  an-vertrauen (*einem etwas*), entrust, confide
  an-wenden (*-wandte, -gewandt*, or weak), apply, use

die Anwesenheit(*-en*), presence
an-zünden, light, ignite
der Apparat(*-e*), camera, apparatus
das Arbeitszimmer(*-*), workroom, study
sich ärgern, be annoyed
der Argwohn, (no pl.), suspicion
der Aristokrat(*-en, -en*), aristocrat
armselig, wretched, miserable, needy
die Art(*-en*), kind, way, manner
arteriosklerotisch, suffering from arterial sclerosis
der Arzt(*⸗e*), doctor
der Ärztekittel(*-*), doctor's (white) coat, overall
die Ärztin(*-nen*), lady doctor
ärztlich, medical, on medical grounds
der Ästhet(*-en, -en*), aesthete, one who appreciates the beautiful
astronomisch, astronomical
atmen, to breathe
die Atomkraft(*⸗e*), atomic power
auf . . . hin, as a result of, in consequence of
auf-atmen, breathe freely, breathe a sigh of relief
auf-bahren, lay out (the dead)
auf-bauen, build up
auf-brechen (*-brach, -gebrochen; sein*), leave, depart
auf-bringen (*-brachte, -gebracht*), get together, scrape together (money); summon up (courage)
auf-decken, uncover
der Aufenthalt(*-e*), stay, sojourn
auf-erstehen (*-erstand, -erstanden; sein*), rise up, rise from the dead
auf-fallen (*-fiel, -gefallen; sein*) (+dat.), strike, occur to (the mind)
auf-fordern, invite, challenge, summon
die Aufforderung(*-en*), request, demand
die Aufgabe(*-n*), task, mission
auf-gehen (*-ging, -gegangen; sein*), go into without a remainder, work out correctly (math.)
aufgeregt, excited
sich auf-halten (*-hielt, -gehalten*), reside, stay
auf-hängen, hang up
auf-heben (*-hob, -gehoben*), keep, preserve, look after; cancel out, annul; lift up
auf-hören, stop, cease
auf-klären, clear up, brighten
auf-kommen (*-kam, -gekommen; sein*), pay (for), be responsible (for)
auf-lachen, laugh out
auf-lesen, pick up
auf-lösen, dissolve
die Aufnahme(*-n*), picture, photo
auf-nehmen (*-nahm, -genommen*), take down; draw up (statement); accept, take up
sich auf-opfern, sacrifice oneself
auf-räumen, tidy up, clear away
sich auf-regen, get excited
auf-reiben (*-rieb, -gerieben*), wear out the nerves, be wearing
auf-reißen (*-riß, -gerissen*), fling open, tear open

auf-saufen (*-soff*, *-gesoffen*), drink up

auf-schließen (*-schloß*, *-geschlossen*), unlock, open up

auf-schreien (*-schrie*, *-geschrien*), scream, shout out

auf-steigen (*-stieg*, *-gestiegen*; *sein*), rise up, arise

auf-stellen, establish (theory); put right (chairs), pick up, set up

sich auf-stellen, take up a position, arrange oneself

auf-suchen, look up, seek out, visit

auf-tauchen, emerge, appear (suddenly)

der *Auftrag*(⸚*e*), order, contract, task

der *Auftraggeber*(*–*), employer, superior

auf-treten (*-trat*, *-getreten*; *sein*), appear, come forward, make an entry

das *Auftreten*, appearance

der *Auftritt*(*–e*), scene, appearance

sich auf-tun, open up

auf-wachen (*sein*), wake up (intrans.)

auf-zeichnen, make notes, sketches

die *Aufzeichnungen* (f. pl.), notes

auf-zwingen (*-zwang*, *-gezwungen*) (*einem etwas*), force upon

das *Auge*(*-es*, *-n*), eye; *ins — fassen*, take into consideration; *im — haben*, bear in mind

aus-arbeiten, work out, complete

aus-bauen, extend, complete

aus-beuten, exploit

sich aus-breiten, spread out, extend

der *Ausdruck*(⸚*e*), expression

aus-drücken, express; squeeze out

aus-erwählen, choose, pick out

der *Ausgangspunkt*(*-e*), starting-point, point of departure

ausgebaut, extensive

sich aus-geben (*-gab*, *-gegeben*) *für*, pass oneself off as

aus-gehen (*-ging*, *-gegangen*; *sein*) *von*, start from

ausgezeichnet, splendid, first-class

aus-klammern, ignore, forget about

aus-kommen (*-kam*, *-gekommen*; *sein*) *mit*, get on with, manage with

die *Auskunft*(⸚*e*), information

aus-liefern (*einem etwas*), hand over, deliver up

aus-löschen (trans., weak), extinguish, put out; obliterate

aus-löschen (*-lischt*, *-losch*, *-geloschen*; *sein*), go out, be extinguished (intrans.)

aus-nützen, exploit, use up, exhaust

die *Aussage*(*-n*), statement, deposition

aus-saufen (*-soff*, *-gesoffen*), drink dry

ausschließlich, exclusively

aus-sehen (*-sah*, *-gesehen*), look, seem, appear

außen, outside, on the outside

die *Außenwelt*, outside world

außerdem, besides

außerhalb (+gen.), outside, beyond
äußern, express, utter
außerordentlich, extraordinary
äußerst, extremely; *das Äußerste*, the utmost
sich aus-setzen (+dat.), expose oneself to
die Aussicht(-en), view, prospect; *in—stehen (stand, gestanden)*, be in the offing; *in—stellen*, hold out a prospect of
aus-spielen, play out, finish
aus-spionieren, spy out, on
die Ausstattung(-en), equipment, fittings, fitting-out, décor
aus-sterben (-starb, -gestorben; sein), die off, out; become extinct
aus-wählen, select
der Ausweg(-e), way out, loophole
ausweichen (-wich, -gewichen; sein) (+dat.), avoid, dodge
ausweichend, evasive
auswendig, by heart
aus-werten, get full value from, exploit
die Auswirkung(-en), effect, consequence
die Autochthonen (pl.), indigenous peoples, races
der Automat(-en, -en), automaton

bahnen, make open (a way), pave (a way)
der Bann, constraint, charm, spell; *in — halten (hielt, gehalten)*, keep in check
barbarisch, barbarian, crude(ly)

der Basedow, goitre (see note, p. 104)
beachten, take notice of
der Beamte (adj. noun), official
das Bedauern, regret, sorrow
bedecken, cover
bedenken (bedachte, bedacht), consider, think over; bequeath
das Bedenken, scruple, consideration
bedenklich, serious, critical
bedeutend, significant(ly), markedly
bedienen, serve
die Bedingung(-en), condition
beeindrucken, impress
beenden, finish, end
der Befehl(-e), order
befehlen (befahl, befohlen) (+dat.), order
sich befinden (befand, befunden), be situated, be
befolgen, obey, follow
befreundet, friendly
der Befund(-e), finding, report
befürchten, fear
begabt, gifted, talented
begegnen (sein) (+dat.), meet
begehen (beging, begangen), commit
begehren, desire, long for
begleiten, accompany
begreifen (begriff, begriffen), grasp, understand
begreiflich, understandable, comprehensible
begründen, substantiate
der Begründer(-), founder
die Begrüssung(-en), greeting, welcome
begutachten, give an opinion on, certify

behandeln, manage, treat
die *Behandlung(-en)*, treatment
behängt, hung (with), decorated (with)
behaupten, assert, maintain
sich *beherrschen*, control oneself
die *Behörde* (sing.), authorities
behutsam, careful(ly)
bei (+dat.), in the case of, with, at
bei-bringen (-brachte, -gebracht) (einem etwas), teach, show
bei-kommen (-kam, -gekommen; sein) (+dat.), get at
beinahe, almost
beisammen, together
das *Beispiel(-e)*, example; *zum —* for example, e.g.
beißen (biß, gebissen), bite
bei-steuern, contribute
bekannt, known
sich *beklagen*, complain
beklagenswert, lamentable
belastet, burdened, encumbered
beleidigen, insult
bemerken, notice
bemerkenswert, distinctly, noticeably
die *Bemerkung(-en)*, remark, note, annotation
sich *bemühen*, busy oneself, be busy; take care
benachrichtigen, inform
benötigen, need
beobachten, observe
bequem, comfortable, comfortably
bereit, ready
bereiten, cause; get ready
bereit-stellen, provide, put ready

der *Beruf(-e)*, profession, job
beruhigen, pacify, soothe; *sich —*, calm oneself down, recover
berühmt, famous
bescheiden, modest, unassuming
beschützen, protect
beseitigen, do away with, get rid of
besichtigen, inspect
besingen (besang, besungen), sing of, about
besitzen (besaß, besessen), possess
die *Besoldung(-en)*, payment, salary
besonders, especially
besprechen (besprach, besprochen), discuss, talk over
bestätigen, confirm; *sich —*, be confirmed, prove to be true
das *Besteck(-e)*, knife, fork, and spoon; cutlery
bestehen auf (+dat.), insist on; *— aus, in*, consist of
bestialisch, beastly, frightful(ly)
bestimmbar, determinable, predictable
bestimmen, determine
bestimmt, definitely
bestrafen, punish
bestückt, set out (with), planted (with)
bestürzt, dismayed, nonplussed
betäuben, drug, stupefy
betrachten, regard, look at
beträchtlich, considerable, considerably

VOCABULARY

das Betragen, behaviour
betreffen (betraf, betroffen), concern, affect
betreten (betrat, betreten) (+ acc.), enter, walk in
betreuen, take care of
beunruhigen, worry, disturb
bevölkert, populated, inhabited
bevormunden, put under a guardian, hold in tutelage
bewachen, to guard
die Bewachung(–en), guard, custody
bewahren, keep, preserve
bewaldet, wooded, woody
bewältigen, overcome
bewegen (bewog, bewogen,) persuade, induce
beweisen (bewies, bewiesen), show, prove
die Bewilligung(–en), consent
bezwecken, aim at
biegsam, flexible, supple
das Biest(–er), wild animal, brute
bieten (bot, geboten) (einem etwas), to offer
das Bild(–er), picture
bilden, constitute, compose
bisweilen, now and again, at times
bitter, bitter(ly)
blättern, turn over leaves, pages
blauschimmernd, with a blue glimmer
bleiben lassen (ließ, gelassen), ignore, forget about
bleich, pale
der Bleidampf(⸚e), lead vapour
blenden, dazzle, blind
das Blitzlicht(–er), flash-light

blitzsauber, very clean, spotless
der Blödsinn, nonsense
blutig, bloody
der Boden(⸚), ground, soil
bösartig, ill-natured, malicious
der Boxhandschuh(–e), boxing-glove
die Brahmssonate(–n), sonata by Brahms (see note, p. 97)
brauchbar, useful
brauchen, need
brav, worthy, good
breiten, spread
der Briefwechsel, correspondence
brüllen, roar
brummen, growl, grumble
brüten, brood, mope
der Bube(–n, –n), boy
bucklig, hump-backed
die Bühne(–n), stage
der Burgunder, Burgundy wine
der Bursche (–n, –n), fellow
büßen, atone for, suffer for

die Chance(–n), chance; *um der — willen*, for the sake of the chance
die Chefärztin(–nen), lady doctor-in-charge

dagegen, on the other hand
daher, therefore
dahin, away, gone, finished
dahinter, behind (it), at the back of
dahinter kommen (–kam, –gekommen; sein), get to the bottom of
der Damenringverein(–e), ladies' wrestling club

dämmern, grow dark, grow dusk; dawn (also fig.=on the mind)
dampfen, steam
dar-stellen, portray, represent
das *Dasein*, existence
da-sein, be, exist
dauern, last
davon-kommen (*-kam, -gekommen; sein*), escape
debil, debilitated, weak
der *Deckel*(–), lid, cover
definitiv, final, definite
deiner, (pron. gen.), of you; — *würdig*, worthy of you
demnach, consequently, accordingly
denkbar, thinkable, conceivable
der *Denkfehler*(–), error in thinking
derjenige, that one, the one
derselbe, the same
deshalb, therefore, on that account
deuten auf (+acc.), point to, indicate; interpret
deutlich, clear, evident
dienen (+dat.), serve
die *Dienerin*(*–nen*), maidservant
der *Dienst*(*–e*), service
die *Dirne*(*–n*), prostitute, wench
diskutieren, discuss
die *Dissertation*(*–en*), dissertation, treatise
doch, yet, nevertheless, after all
donnern, thunder, roar
die *Dosis* (*Dosen*), dose
das *Dossier*(*–s*), dossier, file of papers on one subject
drängen, push, press

draußen, outside
drehen, turn
dringen (*drang, gedrungen*), penetrate, press into; urge
dringend, pressing, urgent(ly)
die *Drogen* (f. pl.), drugs, medicines
drohen (+dat.), threaten
drollig, funny
drüben, over there
dumpf, hollow, muffled (sound); dull
durchaus, absolutely, completely; — *nicht*, not at all, by no means
durch-bringen (*-brachte, -gebracht*), support (family, etc.)
durcheinander, confused, in confusion
durcheinander-bringen (*-brachte, -gebracht*), bring into confusion
durcheinander-geraten (*-geriet, -geraten; sein*), fall into confusion
durcheinander-kommen (*-kam, -gekommen; sein*), get into confusion
durchschauen, see through, find out about
durchziehen (*-zog, -gezogen*), cross, interlace
dürfen, be allowed; may, must, ought
düster, dark, gloomy

eben, just
die *Ebene*(*–n*), plain
ebenfalls, likewise, just as
ebenso, likewise, just as
die *Ehe*(*–n*), marriage

ehemalig, former
eher, earlier, rather
die *Ehre(–n),* honour, respect; *in Ehren,* with all deference to
das *Ehrenwort(⸗er),* word of honour
die *Eichentür(–en),* oak door
eidgenössisch, federal, of the Swiss Federation
eigentlich, proper, true; strictly speaking, actually
eilen, hurry; *sich —,* make haste
eilig, hastily, hurriedly
sich *ein-bilden,* imagine, fancy
ein-brechen (-brach, -gebrochen; sein), break into
eindeutig, clearly, plainly
eindringlich, penetratingly, insistently, urgently
einfach, simple, simply
ein-fallen (-fiel, -gefallen; sein), occur to (mind); strike
sich *ein-fühlen,* have an understanding of, feeling for; adapt oneself to
der *Eingang(⸗e),* entrance
eingebildet, imaginary
ein-gehen (-ging, -gegangen; sein) (+acc.), take (risk); *— auf* (+acc.), enter into the spirit of, agree to
eingesponnen, wrapped up, cocooned
ein-halten (-hielt, -gehalten), observe, adhere to
die *Einheit(–en),* unity
einheitlich, uniform
einig sein über, be agreed on
ein-laden (-lud, -geladen), invite
sich *ein-leben,* settle in, settle down
ein-liefern, deliver into, hand over to
ein-nehmen (-nahm, -genommen), eat, consume
sich *ein-puppen,* wrap oneself up (fig.), cocoon oneself in
die *Einsamkeit,* loneliness
ein-schenken, pour in, fill up (a glass)
sich *ein-schiffen,* embark
ein-schlafen (-schlief, -geschlafen; sein), fall asleep
ein-schleichen (-schlich, -geschlichen; sein), creep, sneak into
ein-schreiten (-schritt, -geschritten; sein), step in, interfere
ein-sehen (-sah, -gesehen), see, realize, grasp
ein-setzen, put into operation, action; use; *sich — für,* stand up for, give aid to
die *Einsicht(–en),* insight, realization
ein-sperren, lock up
einst, once, one time
ein-stecken, put in (the pocket)
einstweilen, meanwhile
ein-treten (-trat, -getreten; sein), enter
einverstanden, in agreement
die *Einzelzelle(–n),* single cell
einzig, only
das *Elementarteilchen(–),* elementary particle
die *Elite(–n),* elite
empfehlen (empfahl, empfohlen) (einem etwas), recommend; *— lassen bei,* give regards to
die *Empfehlung(–en),* recommendation
endgültig, final(ly), definite; irrevocably

endlich, finally, at last
der Engel(-), angel
entdecken, discover
der Entdecker(-), discoverer
die Entdeckung(-en), discovery
sich entfernen, withdraw, go away
entführen, abduct, kidnap
entgegen-starren (+ dat.), stare towards
enthüllen, reveal, uncover
entkommen (*entkam, entkommen; sein*), escape
entlang (+acc. or preceded by *an* +dat.), along
entscheiden (*entschied, entschieden*), decide; *sich—*, make up one's mind
die Entscheidung(-en), decision
sich entschließen (*entschloß, entschlossen*), decide
der Entschluß(∺sse), decision
entschuldigen, excuse
entsprechen (*entsprach, entsprochen*) (+ dat.), correspond to, accord with
entsprechend, corresponding(ly)
die Entsprechungslehre(-n), theory of correspondences (see note, p. 102)
entstammen, spring from, be descended from
entwaffnen, disarm
entwickeln, develop
die Epoche(-n), epoch, period
erbarmen, move to pity; *sich —* (gen.), take pity on
erblich, hereditary
erblicken, catch sight of, see
erdrosseln, strangle
sich ereignen, occur, take place, happen

erfahren (*erfuhr, erfahren*), learn, find out
erfaßbar, comprehensible, understandable
erfinden (*erfand, erfunden*), invent, discover
die Erfindung(-en), discovery, intention
der Erfolg(-e), success
erfolglos, unsuccessfully
erfreut, pleased, delighted
erfrieren (*erfror, erfroren; sein*), freeze to death, be numb with cold
ergreifen (*ergriff, ergriffen*), grasp, comprehend
ergriffen, moved, touched
erhaben, exalted, sublime
erhalten (*erhielt, erhalten*), receive; preserve
sich erheben (*erhob, erhoben*), get up, stand up
sich erinnern an (+ acc.), remember
erkennbar, recognizable, discernible, comprehensible
erkennen (*erkannte, erkannt*), recognize
die Erkenntnis(-se), knowledge, cognition, perception
die Erklärung(-en), explanation
erkranken (*sein*), fall ill, become ill
erledigen, settle, execute, carry out
erleuchten, illuminate
erlöschen (*erlischt, erlosch, erloschen; sein*), die out, become extinct
ermöglichen, make possible
ermorden, murder
sich ernähren, be sustained by, live on

erobern, conquer
eröffnen, disclose, reveal
erregt, moved, touched
erreichen, reach
errichten, establish
erröten, blush
erscheinen (erschien, erschienen; sein) (prep. +dat.), appear
das Erscheinen, appearance
die Erscheinung(-en), apparition, phenomenon, appearance
erschöpft, worn out, exhausted
erschrecken (weak, trans.), frighten, scare
erschrecken (erschrak, erschrocken; sein), be frightened
erst, first, not till, only
erstaunen, astonish, surprise
erstehen (erstand, erstanden), buy, acquire
ertragen (ertrug, ertragen), bear, tolerate
erträglich, tolerable, bearable
erwähnen, mention
erweisen (erwies, erwiesen), prove, show
erzählen, tell, relate
erzittern, shake, tremble
der Esel(-), donkey, ass, fool
das Etui(-s), case (cigarettes, cigars)
ewig, eternal; *auf* —, for ever

die Fabrik(-en), factory
die Fachsimpelei(-en), talking shop
das Fachsimpeln, talking shop
fähig, capable
fahrbereit, ready to go
fahren-lassen (ließ, gelassen), let go, give up
die Fakultät(-en), faculty
der Fall(≃e), case

fällen, make, give (decree, verdict)
fällig, due
falls, in case
das Familientreffen, family meeting, reunion
fassen, apprehend, seize, grasp
fassunglos, uncomprehending; disconcerted
fehlen (+dat.), be lacking, missing
der Fehler(-), error
der Fehlschluß(≃sse), wrong conclusion, deduction
feierlich, solemn(ly)
das Fenster(-), window
die Fensterfront(-en), expanse of windows
ferner, furthermore
fertig, ready, finished; *das macht mich* —, wears me out
fest, firm(ly)
fest-stellen, determine, ascertain, notice
das Feuer(-), fire; *haben Sie* —?, have you a light?
fiedeln, fiddle
der Fingerabdruck(≃e), fingerprint
flankieren, flank
die Flasche(-n), bottle
flehen um, beseech for, implore
fliehen (floh, geflohen; sein), flee
die Flöte(-n), flute
das Flötenspiel, flute playing
der Fluch(≃e), curse, oath
die Flucht(-en), flight
sich flüchten vor (+dat.), flee from, take refuge from
der Fluchtversuch(-e), attempted escape
die Flügeltür(-en), double door, swing-door

der Fluß(⸗sse), river, stream
flüstern, whisper
die Folge(-n), consequence
der Fond(-s), fund
fordern, demand, ask
die Formel, formula
die Forschung(-en), research
fort, away, off
der Fortgang(⸗e), progress, advance
fort-schaffen, remove
fort-schicken, send away, off
der Fortschritt(-e), progress
der Frack(-s or ⸗e), frock-coat, dress-coat
die Fratze(-n), grimace; mug, dial (slang for 'face')
die Frauenabteilung(-en), women's ward
die Freiheit(-en), freedom
frei-setzen, free, set free
freiwillig, voluntary, voluntarily
die Freizeit, spare time, leisure
fressen (fraß, gefressen), eat (of animals)
freudig, joyful(ly)
sich freuen (+gen., or *über* +acc.), be glad about
der Friede(n), *(-ns, -n)*, peace
friedlich, peaceful
fromm, pious, devout, holy
fruchtbar, fertile, fruitful
frühreif, precocious
fühlen, feel
führen, lead, run
fünfzehnjährig, 15-year-old
funkeln, sparkle, twinkle
fürchten, fear; *sich — vor* (+dat.), be afraid of
der Fürst(-en, -en), prince
füttern, feed

die Gage(-n), wage, salary
ganz, whole, altogether
gar, absolutely, even; cooked; *— nicht*, not at all
der Gatte(-n, -n), husband
die Gattin(-nen), wife
das Gebäude(-), building
das Gebiet(-e), district, region, sphere
der Gebirgszug(⸗e), range of mountains
geboren, born
der Geburtstag(-e), birthday
das Gedächtnis(-se), memory
der Gedanke(-ns, -n), thought
geeignet, suited, adapted
die Gefahr(-en), danger
gefährden, endanger
gefährlich, dangerous
gefallen (gefiel, gefallen) (+ dat.), please
der Gefangene (adj. noun), prisoner
das Gefängnis(-se), prison
das Gefüge(-), structure
das Gefühl(-e), feeling
das Gegeige, fiddling (coll.)
gegen (+acc.), against; *gegen ... zu*, towards
die Gegend(-en), district
der Gegensatz(⸗e), contrast; *im Gegensatze zu*, in contrast to, with
das Gegenteil(-e), contrary, reverse; *im —*, on the contrary
die Gegenwart(-en), present time, present
der Gegner(-), opponent
geheim, secret
der Geheimdienst(-e), Secret Service

geheim-halten (hielt, -gehalten), keep secret

das Geheimnis(-se), secret

geheimnisvoll, mysterious

der Geheimrat(⸚e), privy councillor

der Geheimsender(-), secret transmitter

gehen (ging, gegangen; sein), go, walk; *das geht nicht*, that's impossible; *es geht um (+ acc.)*, ... is at stake

das Gehirn(-e), brain

gehorchen (+ dat.), obey

gehören (+ dat.), belong; — *zu*, be among, be one of; belong to

die Geige(-n), fiddle, violin

geigen, play the fiddle, violin

das Geigen, fiddling

der Geigenbogen(⸚), bow

das Geigenspiel(-e), fiddling, violin playing

der Geisteskranke (adj. noun), lunatic

der Geisteszustand(⸚e), mental condition

geistig, mental, intellectual

das Gelächter, laughter

gelangen (sein), reach, arrive at (+ prep.)

gelb, yellow

gelegen: mir liegt viel daran; mir ist daran —, I am very interested in that, concerned about it

die Gelegenheit(-en), opportunity (*zu*, for); occasion

der (die) Geliebte (adj. noun), lover, sweetheart

gelten (galt, gegolten) für, pass for

gemächlich, comfortable, easy-going

die Gemeinde(-n), community, district

die Gemeindeschwester(-n), district nurse

gemeinsam, together, in common

die Gemeinschaft(-en), community

das Gemüt(-er), mind, spirit

gemütlich, affable, jovial, cosy

genannt, called, named

die Genauigkeit, accuracy

der Generaldirektor(-en, -en), managing director

der Generalfeldmarschall(⸚e), field-marshal

der Generalstab(⸚e), general staff

genial, gifted, having genius, original

das Genie(-s), genius

genießen (genoß, genossen), to enjoy

der Genuß(⸚sse), enjoyment, pleasure

gepolstert, padded, upholstered

das Gepolter(-), din, racket

gerade, just

gerade zu, absolutely, frankly

das Gerät(-e), instrument, apparatus

geraten (geriet, geraten; sein), get, fall into (rage, etc.)

das Geräusch(-e), noise

gerecht, just

die Gerechtigkeit, justice

das Gericht(-e), court of justice; commandment; dish

der Gerichtsmediziner(-), police doctor, court doctor

gering, small, slight

das Geschäft(-e), business, firm
geschehen (geschah, geschehen; sein), happen
gescheitert, wrecked, frustrated ruined
geschieden, divorced
das Geschirr(-e), crockery, table utensils, dishes
geschlagen, defeated
das Gesetz(-e), law
das Gesicht(-er), face
gespannt, eager, keen, curious, strained
gespenstig, ghost-like, ghostly
das Gespräch(-e), conversation
das Geständnis(-se), confession, admission
gestatten, allow, permit
gestehen (gestand, gestanden), confess
gestrichen (p.p. of *streichen*), painted
gesund, healthy
gesundheitlich, appertaining to health
das Getriebe(-), bustle, busy world
gewachsen (+ dat.), equal to, a match for
gewaltig, powerful, big, vast
gewiß, certain
das Gewissen(-), conscience
der Gips(-e), plaster
das Gitter(-), grille, barred frame, grating, screen
der Glanz, splendour, glory
das Gläschen, small glass
die Glasmalerei(-en), work in stained glass
der Glaube(-ns, -n), belief; faith
glauben, believe
gleich, same
gleichen (glich, geglichen) (+ dat.), resemble
gleichgültig, indifferent
gleich-kommen (-kam, -gekommen; sein), amount to the same, be the same as
gleichwohl, none the less
gleichzeitig, at the same time
die Glocke(-n), bell
glotzen, stare, gape
das Glück, happiness, luck
glücklich, happy
die Glühbirne(-n), electric light bulb
der Goldrahmen(-), gold frame
der Gottesfriede(-ns, -n), peace in God
die Gottesfurcht, piety
gottesfürchtig, pious
das Grab(̈er), grave
sich grämen, grieve, worry
gräßlich, frightful, horrible, monstrous
gratulieren (einem zu etwas), congratulate
graugrünlich, grey-green
grausam, cruel(ly)
die Gravitation, gravity, gravitation
greifen (griff, gegriffen) nach (+ dat.), grasp at, for
grell, dazzling, bright(ly)
die Grenze(-n), frontier
großartig, excellent, magnificent, splendid
der Großbetrieb(-e), large concern
der Großindustrielle (adj. noun), captain of industry, industrial magnate
grübeln, ponder, brood
der Grund(̈e), reason
der Grundbeziehung(-en), basic relationship

gründen, found
der Gründer(-), founder
die Gründerin(-nen), founder
die Grundlage(-n), basis, foundation
grundlos, without foundation, without reason
das Grüppchen(-), little group
die Gruppe(-n), group
die Gunst(-bezeigungen), favour, grace; *zu Gunsten* (+ gen.), in favour of
günstig, favourable
das Gutachten, (expert) judgement, advice, opinion
der Gymnasiast(-en, -en), grammar-school boy

hacken, hoe, chop, mince
hager, haggard, thin
der Hahn(ⁿe), cock
die Halle(-n), hall
sich halten (hielt, gehalten) für, consider (oneself) to be, consider as
die Haltung(-en), behaviour, attitude
hämmern, hammer, knock
der Handel(ⁿ), trade, commerce
handeln, act, behave; *es handelt sich um* (+acc.), it's a question of
die Handelsschule(-n), trade school, technical school
die Handlung(-en), action, plot (of play)
das Handtuch(ⁿer), towel
hangen (hing, gehangen; intrans.), hang
harmlos, harmless
hassen, hate
die Haube(-n), hood, cap

der Haudegen(-), warrior
das Hauptgebäude(-), main building
die Hauptsache(-n), main thing, essential
hausen, live, dwell
heben (hob, gehoben), lift, raise
heftig, violent, fervent
die Heilanstalt(-en), hospital, sanatorium
heilig, holy, sacred
heiraten, marry
heiß, hot
heißen (hieß, geheißen), be called, be a question of, be the time for; tell, bid
der Held(-en, -en), hero
der Heldentod, heroic death
helfen (half, geholfen) (+dat.), help
hemmungslos, unrestrainedly, without restraint
der Henker(-), hangman, executioner
die Henkersmahlzeit(-en), last meal (before death), hangman's meal (see note, p. 102)
heran-kommen (-kam, -gekommen; *sein) an* (+acc.), get at, get hold of
heran-schweben, go up to in hovering flight
sich heraus-stellen, turn out
herrschen, reign, prevail, govern
her-stellen, set up, make, manufacture
herum-stapfen, pace, trudge round
herunter-reichen, reach down to
herunter-reißen (-riß, -gerissen), tear down

hervor-holen (*hinter* + dat.), take out (from behind)
hervor-ziehen (*-zog, -gezogen*), pull out
das *Herz*(*-ens, -en*), heart
hetzen, chase after, hound; incite; set upon
das *Heu*, hay
heute, today
heutig, present, of today
hienieden, down here, on earth
der *Himmel*(*-*), sky, heaven(s)
hinaus-schaffen, take out, remove
hinaus-tragen (*trug, getragen*), carry out
hinein-steigen (*-stieg, -gestiegen; sein*), climb in, get in
die *Hingabe*(*-n*), devotion, surrender
der *Hintergrund*(*⸚e*), background
hinterlassen (*hinterließ, hinterlassen*), leave behind
hinunter-fiedeln, fiddle to the end, fiddle through
sich *hinunter-lassen* (*-ließ, -gelassen*), reach down (to), extend (to)
hinunter-reichen, reach down to
der *Hirt*(*e*)(*-n*), *-n*), shepherd
hoffen, hope
der *Hofstaat*(*-en*), court splendour
holen, fetch
die *Horde*(*-n*), horde
horrend, dreadful
human, humane
der *Hut*(*⸚e*), hat
hygienisch, hygienic

immens, immense, marvellous
immer noch, still
immerhin, nevertheless
immerzu, always, continually
indem, whilst, as
der *Inhalt*, content(s)
inne-halten (*-hielt, -gehalten*), stop, pause (in speaking)
innen, within, inside
innerlich, inward(ly), mental(ly)
innert, within (coll.)
innig, heartfelt, ardent, fervent (see note, p. 99)
die *Insulinkur*(*-en*), insulin treatment
interniert, interned, confined
inwiefern, to what extent
inzwischen, meanwhile
irgendwo, somewhere
der *Irre* (adj. noun), mad person, lunatic
die *Irrenärztin*(*-nen*), (lady) psychiatrist, doctor for mental patients
das *Irrenhaus*(*⸚er*), lunatic asylum
der *Irrenwärter*(*-*), asylum warder
der *Irrtum*(*⸚er*), error, mistake

das *Jahrhundert*(*-e*), century
jährlich, yearly
jämmerlich, miserable, wretched(ly)
je . . . desto, the more . . . the more
jedenfalls, at any rate, in any case
jedermann, everyone
jederzeit, at any time
jedoch, however
jemals, ever, at any time
jemand, someone, anyone
jubeln, cheer, rejoice
der *Jude*(*-n, -n*), Jew
der *Judoverband*(*⸚e*), judo league, club

VOCABULARY

die Jungfer(-n), virgin, maid
die Jungfrau(-en), virgin, maid
jungfräulich, virginal

der Kamin(-e), fireplace
das Kamingitter(-), fire-screen
der Kaminschirm(-e), fire-screen
der (das) Kaminsims(-e), mantlepiece
der Kampf(ӫe), fight, struggle
der Kanzler(-), chancellor
die Kapelle(-n), chapel, orchestra
kapieren, grasp, understand
die Kapitulation, surrender
kärglich, scanty, scarce
die Karriere(-n), career (French)
die Kassettendecke(-n), inlaid ceiling (see note, p. 96).
kategorisch, categorically, unconditionally
kauern, crouch, cower
kaum, scarcely, hardly
der Kaviar, caviare
keinesfalls, in no case, under no circumstances
kennen-lernen, get to know
der Kerl(-e), fellow
der Kernphysiker(-), nuclear physicist
die Kerze(-n), candle
kinderreich, having many children, prolific
die Kiste(-n), box
die Klause(-n), den, cell, closet
die Klavierbegleitung(-en), piano accompaniment
das Klavierspiel, piano playing
die Klimaanlage, air-conditioning plant
der Knabe(-n, -n), (-n), boy

der Koffer(-), case, suitcase
die Kognakflasche(-n), cognac bottle
der Kollege(-n, -n), colleague
der Koloß(-sse), colossus, giant
kommen (kam, gekommen; sein) auf (+acc.), hit upon
das Kompendium(-ien), guide, handbook; summary
konsumieren, consume, drink
der Kontakt(-e), contact
die Körperfülle, plumpness, corpulence
der Koryphäe(-n), star, celebrity (see note, p. 105)
die Kosten (pl.), costs
das Kostüm(-e), costume, fancy dress
kostümiert, dressed, uniformed
kotzen, vomit, spew
die Kraft(ӫe), strength, force
kräftig, strong, powerful
krähen, screech, crow
die Krankenschwester(-n), nurse
das Krankenzimmer(-), sick-room, patient's room
die Krankheitsgeschichte(-n), case-history
der Kranz(ӫe), wreath
kraß, crass, flagrant, utterly
kreisen, orbit, turn
die Kreutzersonate, Kreutzer sonata (see note, p. 96)
kreuzbrav, extremely good, thoroughly honest
kriegen, get, obtain (coll.)
der Kriminalbeamte (**adj. noun**)**,** detective
der Kriminalinspektor(-en), detective inspector
kriminell, criminal, culpable
der Kronleuchter(-), chandelier

kulinarisch, culinary, appertaining to the kitchen
sich kümmern um, bother about, care for
die Kunst(⁼e), art, skill
kurzentschloßen, abruptly, with quick decision

lächerlich, ridiculous
die Lackfarbe(-n), enamel paint
laden (lud, geladen), load
die Lage(-n), situation, position
das Lamm(⁼er), lamb
die Lampenschnur(⁼e or -en), lamp flex, cable
die Landesmeisterin(-nen), women's national champion
die Landesverteidigung, national defence
die Landschaft(-en), scenery, landscape
landwirtschaftlich, agricultural
lauern, lie in wait, lurk
lauten, sound, run, read (intrans.)
läuten, ring
lautlos, mute, silent(ly)
das Lavabo(-s), wash-basin
leben, live; — *Sie wohl*, farewell
lebenslänglich, lifelong, for life
das Leder, leather
das Leere (adj. noun), void, emptiness (more often *die Leere*)
die Leiche(-n), corpse
die Leichtindustrie(-n), light industry
das Leid(en), harm, hurt; *es tut mir leid*, I am sorry
das Leiden, suffering
leidenschaftlich, passionate, enthusiastic

leider, unfortunately
leisten, achieve, perform; *sich* — (+acc.), afford
leiten, lead, conduct, manage
lenkbar, docile
lenken, guide, direct
leuchten, light, shine
licht, light, bright
der Lichtstrahl(-en), ray (of light)
liebenswert, lovable, likeable
das Liebesleid(-en), love's sorrow
liefern, deliver, hand over
liegen (lag, gelegen), lie, be situated
die Lippe(-n), lip
loben, praise
das Loch(⁼er), hole
logisch, logical(ly)
los, loose, free
los-lassen (-ließ, -gelassen) auf (+acc.), let loose on
löschen, extinguish
lösen, solve, loosen
die Lösung(-en), solution
lügen (log, gelogen), lie, tell a lie
die Lust(⁼e), desire, pleasure, inclination
der Lüster(-), chandelier
die Macht(⁼e), power, might
machtlos, powerless
die Machtmittel (n. pl.), means of power, access to power
der Machtpolitiker(-), power politician
mächtig, mighty, powerful
die Magd(⁼e), maid
die Mahlzeit(-en), meal
majestätisch, majestic(ally)
das Mal(-e), time; *mit einem* —, all at once
mangeln (impers.), be lacking, wanting

VOCABULARY

die Manneshöhe, height of a man
die Mannschaft(*-en*), team
mannshoch, as high as a man
die Mansarde(*-n*), attic
der Mantel(*⸚*), overcoat, gown
die Mappe(*-n*), letter-case, portfolio, music-case
maskenhaft, like a mask
die Materie(*-n*), matter, substance
die Mauer(*-n*), wall
mehrere, several
meinen, think
meinerseits, for my part, on my side
die Meinung(*-en*), opinion; *meiner — nach*, in my opinion
das Meißnerporzellan, Dresden china (see note, p. 101)
meistens, mostly
der Meister(*-*), champion
der Meisterboxer(*-*), boxing champion
melden, announce; *sich —*, report, come forward
der Mensch(*-en, -en*), human being
der Menschenfreund(*-e*), philanthropist
die Menschheit, mankind
menschlich, human
merkwürdig, remarkable, significant, strange
messen (*maß, gemessen*), measure
der Methanbrei, methane brew, broth
das Metier(*-s*), trade, profession (French)
die Miene(*-n*), countenance, mien, expression
mieten, rent

mißbrauchen, misuse
der Missionar(*-e*), missionary
die Missionsstation(*-en*), missionary station
mißtrauisch, mistrusting(ly)
mißverstehen (*mißverstand, mißverstanden*), misunderstand
das Mitglied(*-er*), member
die Mitte(*-n*), middle
mit-teilen (*einem etwas*), inform
das Mittel(*-*), remedy; (pl.), means, resources
das Mittelgewicht, middle-weight
mittler, medium, average
mittlerweile, meanwhile
das Möbel(*-*), (piece of) furniture
mögen, like, may; *ich möchte*, I should like
möglich, possible
die Möglichkeit(*-en*), possibility
der Monat(*-e*), month
der Mond(*-e*), moon
das Moor(*-e*), bog, fen
moralisch, morally
der Mord(*-e*), murder
morden, murder
das Morden, murdering
der Mörder(*-*), murderer
mörderisch, murderous
der Mordfall(*⸚e*), murder case
die Mumie(*-n*), mummy
der Musterpatient(*-en, -en*), model patient
der Mut, courage
mutig, courageous
mutlos, timid, cowardly
die Mütze(*-n*), cap

nach-denken *-dachte, -gedacht*)
  über (+ acc.), reflect, ponder
nachdenklich, thoughtful(ly)

nach-forschen, search after, investigate into
nach-geben (*-gab*, *-gegeben*), yield, give in
nach-kommen (*-kam*, *-gekommen*; *sein*), follow on, after
nach-krähen, crow after, crow about
die Nachricht(–en), news
nach-schreien(–schrie, –geschrieen), shout after
nach-sehen (*-sah, -gesehen*), look after, into
die Nächstenliebe, love of one's neighbour
der Nacken(–), nape, back of neck
nackt, naked
die Nähe(–n), neighbourhood, vicinity
näher, nearer, more detailed
namenlos, nameless
nämlich, for, you see
der Narr(–en, –en), fool
die Narrenkappe(–n), fool's cap
die Naturbeobachtung(–en), observation of nature
die Naturwissenschaft(–en), science
der Neger(–), Negro
neidisch, envious (*auf* + acc., of)
nennen (*nannte, genannt*), name
nennenswert, worth mentioning, noteworthy
der Nerv(–en), nerve
nervenkrank, suffering from nervous disorder, neurotic
das Nest(–er), nest, small town
nett, nice
der Neubau(–ten), new building
die Neugierde, curiosity
neugierig, curious
nicken, nod

nie, never
nieder-schlagen (*-schlug, -geschlagen*), dishearten, deject
nieder-schreiben (*-schrieb, -geschrieben*), write down
niemand, no one
der Notfall(⸚e), case of emergency
nötig haben, need
das Notizbuch(⸚er), notebook
numerieren, number
nutzlos, useless

ob (+ gen.) on account of; if, whether
oben, above
ober, upper
der Oberpfleger(–), (male) staff nurse
die Oberschwester(–n), matron
obwohl, although
offenbar, obvious(ly)
offenbaren, reveal
die Offenbarung(–en), revelation
die Öffentlichkeit, public, public places
öffnen, open
öfters, several times, often
ohnehin, in any case, besides
die Ölpfütze(–n), pool of oil
das Opfer(–), victim, sacrifice
opfern, to sacrifice
die Optik, optics
der Orden(–), decoration, order
ordnen, order, arrange
die Ordnungsliebe, love of order, tidiness
die Orgel(–n), organ
der Ort(–e), scene, place
das Örtliche (adj. noun), local scene, place
die Ostschweiz, eastern Switzerland

pachten, lease, take a lease of; have a monopoly of
packen, seize; *sich—*, clear off, go away
paffen, puff, smoke; *vor sich hin-paffen*, puff away (deep in thought)
päppeln, coddle
das *Parkett(-e)*, inlaid floor, parquet floor
die *Parkfront(-en)*, French windows (opening on a park)
die *Partei(-en)*, party
die *Partitur(-en)*, musical score
passabel, passable, tolerable, tolerably
das *Patentamt(⸚er)*, patents office
die *Pause(-n)*, break, interval, rest
der *Pavillon(-s)*, pavilion
das *Pech*, bad luck
persönlich, personally
die *Perücke(-n)*, wig
die *Pest(-en)*, plague
der *Pfarrer(-)*, parson
pfeilschnell, quick as an arrow
pflegen, care for, be accustomed to
der *Pfleger(-)*, male nurse
die *Pflegerin(-nen)*, nurse
die *Pflicht(-en)*, duty
der *Philanthrop(-en, -en)*, philanthropist
photokopieren, make photostat copies of
der *Physiker*, physicist
die *Pionierarbeit(-en)*, pioneer work
planmäßig, according to plan
Platz nehmen (nahm, genommen), take a seat
plötzlich, suddenly

der *Politiker(-)*, politician
die *Polizei*, police
der *Polizist(-en, -en)*, policeman
der *Posten(-)*, position, job
prächtig, splendid, magnificent
präzis, precise, exact
der *Prediger(-)*, preacher
preisen (pries, gepriesen), praise
pressen, press
das *Prinzip(-ien)*, principle, method
die *Professur(-en)*, professorship
prüfen, examine, test
der *Psalmendichter(-)*, psalmist
der *Psychiater(-)*, psychiatrist
die *Psychiatrie*, psychiatry
das *Publikum*, public, audience
der *Purpurmantel(⸚)*, purple robe

quälen, torture

die *Rache(-n)*, vengeance
der *Rahmen(-)*, frame
der *Rasen(-)*, lawn
rasend, furious
die *Raserei(-en)*, fury, madness, frenzy
der *Rat(-schläge)*, counsel, advice
ratlos, perplexed, at one's wits' end
der *Ratschlag(⸚e)*, advice
das *Rätsel(-)*, puzzle
rauben, rob
der *Raum(⸚e)*, space, place, room
räumen, clear away
raus! (coll. for *heraus!*), out!
reagieren, react
rechnen, count, consider, reckon; *— mit*, count on, rely on
die *Rechnung(-en)*, account

das Recht(-e), right, privilege
rechts, on the right
rechtzeitig, at the right time, in good time
die Rede(-n), talk, speech
reden, talk, speak
der Redner(-), speaker
regeln, arrange, order
regieren, govern
die Regierung(-en), government
der Rehzwilling(-e), roe twin
das Reich(-e), realm, empire
der Reichtum(⸚er), fortune, wealth
rein, pure
reißen (riß, gerissen), tear
reklamieren, claim, protest
die Relativitätstheorie, theory of relativity
rennen (rannte, gerannt; sein), run
resolut, firm, resolute
richtig, proper(ly), correctly, really
riechen (roch, gerochen), smell, scent (*nach*, of)
riesenhaft, colossal, gigantic
die Riesenkraft(⸚e), gigantic strength
das Riesenwerk(-e), gigantic factory, enormous concern
riesig, gigantic
die Ringerin(-nen), woman wrestler
das Risiko(-s or *-en)*, risk; *ein — ein-gehen (-ging, -gegangen)*, take a risk
robust, robust, healthy
das Röcheln, death-rattle
die Rolle(-n), role, part
rotieren, rotate
der Rückschritt(-e), relapse, regression.

der Ruf(-e), fame, repute; call, shout
die Ruhe(-n), peace, rest
ruhen, rest
ruhig, calm(ly)
der Ruhm, fame
ruinieren, ruin
rund, round
runter, (coll. for *herunter*), down

die Sache(-n), thing, affair, matter; *zur —!* let's get to the point!
der Salon(-s), drawing-room
sämtlich, all, complete, entire
das Sanator-ium(-ien), sanatorium
sanft, gentle, soft
der Sänger(-), singer
das Satyrspiel(-e), satyr play (see note, p. 96)
das Schach, chess
der Schade(n)(-ns, ⸚n), pity, damage
der Schalter, switch
schamlos, shameless(ly), impudent(ly)
scharf, sharp(ly)
der Schatten(-), shadow
schattenhaft, shadowy, indistinct
schätzen, treasure, prize, esteem
die Schatzkammer(-n), treasury
die Scheibe(-n), pane
scheiden (schied, geschieden), separate; *sich — lassen*, get divorced
die Scheidung(-en), separation, divorce
scheinbar, apparently

VOCABULARY

scheinen (*schien, geschienen*), seem; shine
der Scheinwerfer(*-*), searchlight, floodlight
scheitern, become a wreck, fail, be frustrated
scheußlich, frightful, terrible
schicken nach, send for
schicklich, correct, proper
das Schicksal(*-e*), destiny, fate
schieben (*schob, geschoben*), shove, push
schief, crooked, awry, wrong
schießen (*schoß, geschossen*), shoot
schizophren, schizophrenic
die Schläfe(*-n*), temple (of the head)
schlafen (*schlief, geschlafen*), sleep
schlagen (*schlug, geschlagen*), strike
schlemmen, gormandize, carouse, revel
schlendern, saunter, stroll
schleunig, quickly, hastily
schlicht, simple, simply, plain
schließen (*schloß, geschlossen*), close; form (friendship etc.)
schließlich, after all, finally
schlimm, bad, serious
schlimmstmöglich, worst possible
schlohweiß, snow-white
das Schloß(*⸗sser*), castle, lock
der Schlotbaron(*-e*), factory-owner, industrialist
der Schluß(*⸗sse*), conclusion, deduction; — *machen mit*, put an end to
der Schlußstrich(*-e*), final settlement, finish; *einen — unter eine Sache ziehen*, put an end to something
der Schlüssel(*-*), key
schmächtig, slim, slender
schmecken, taste
schmerzlich, painful
schmuck, neat, tidy, pretty
der Schmuck(*-e*), jewellery, decoration
der Schnaps(*⸗e*), spirit, brandy
schnuppern, sniff, snuff; snoop
die Schnur(*⸗e* or *-en*), flex, cable
der Schnurrbart(*⸗e*), moustache
die Schokoladefabrik(*-en*), chocolate factory
schöpfen, conceive, get (suspicions etc.); create; ladle
schrecklich, terrible
der Schreibtisch(*-e*), writing-desk
der Schriftsteller(*-*), writer
der Schritt(*-e*), step
die Schuld(*-en*), guilt, fault
die Schulter(*-n*), shoulder
die Schuppe(*-n*), scale (of fish etc.)
schütteln, shake
schützen vor, protect from
schwach, weak; — *bevölkert*, thinly populated
der Schwächling(*-e*), weakling
schweben, hover, soar, float (in air)
schweigen (*schwieg, geschwiegen*), be silent
schweigsam, silent, taciturn
der Schweiß, sweat
schwerfällig, heavy, ponderous
das Schwergewichtsboxen, heavyweight boxing
die Schwerkraft, gravity
die Schwester(*-n*), nurse; sister
die Schwesterntracht(*-en*), nurse's uniform

schwungvoll, stirring, with gusto
der *See*(*-n*), lake
seelenruhig, composed, quiet
das *Seeufer*(*-*), lakeside
segnen, bless
der *Sekt*, champagne
selber, oneself
selbstverständlich, of course
servieren, serve
der *Sessel*(*-*), easy-chair
sich *setzen*, sit down
sicher, sure(ly)
die *Sicherheit*, certainty, safety, security
die *Sicherheitsmaßnahme*(*-n*), security precaution
sichern, make safe, secure, protect
sichtbar, visible
das *Silberbesteck*(*-e*), silver cutlery
der *Sinn*(*-e*), sense, mind
sinnlos, senseless
sinnwidrig, absurd
das *Sofa*(*-s*), sofa, couch
sogar, even
sollen, shall, to be to, to be supposed to
somit, consequently, accordingly
sommerlich, summerlike, of (in) the summer
das *Sommersitz*(*-e*), summer home, residence
der *Sonnensystem*(*-e*), solar system
sonnig, sunny
sonst, otherwise, normally
die *Sorge*(*-n*), care, worry
sich *sorgen um*, worry about
sortieren, select, sort out
sowas (coll. for *so etwas*), such a thing
sowie, as well as

sparen, save
der *Spaßvogel*(*≃*), joker
der *Specht*(*-e*), woodpecker
sperren, lock, bar
das *Spezialschloß*(*≃sser*), patent lock
die *Spielerei*(*-en*), pastime, frivolity, trifling
der *Spion*(*-e*), spy
spitzbärtig, with pointed beard
der *Spott*, ridicule, scorn
spotten (+ gen., or *über* + acc.), ridicule, deride, scoff at
der *Sprachkurs*(*-e*), language course
der *Sprengstoff*(*-e*), dynamite
der *Sproß*(*-ssen*), offspring, scion
die *Spur*(*-en*), trace; *einem auf die — kommen*, get on the track of
staatlich, State, belonging to the State
der *Staatsanwalt*(*≃e*), public prosecutor
die *Stadt*(*≃e*), town
stammen von (or *aus*), come from, stem from, originate from
stampfen, stamp
der *Stand*(*≃e*), position; *im Stande sein*, be in a position to
stand-halten (*-hielt, -gehalten*) (+ dat.), stand up to, resist
der *Standpunkt*(*-e*), standpoint
die *Stange*(*-e*), rod, pole, stick
stapfen, stamp, pace
starr, stiff, rigid, staring
starren, stare; *vor sich hinstarren*, stare into space
statt-finden (*-fand, gefunden*), take place

VOCABULARY

der Staub, dust
   stecken, stick, put, insert
   stehen (*stand, gestanden*), stand, be situated
   stehen-bleiben (*-blieb, geblieben; sein*), stop, halt
die Stehlampe(*-n*), standard lamp
das Steingeländer(*-*), stone railing, balustrade
die Steinmauer(*-n*), stone wall
die Stelle(*-n*), place, position
die Stellung(*-en*), position, post
   stemmen, weight-lift, lift weights
der Stenoblock(*⸚e*), writing-pad
   stenografieren, write shorthand
der Sterne(*-e*), star
   steuern, steer
der Stich(*-e*), prick, sting, stitch; *im — lassen* (*ließ, gelassen*), leave in the lurch
die Stiftung(*-en*), endowment, bequest, foundation
   still, peaceful, quiet; *der Stille Ozean*, Pacific Ocean
die Stille(*-n*), stillness, quiet, silence
   stimmen, be correct; be true, in order
   stinken (*stank, gestunken*), stink
die Stirne(*-n*), brow, forehead
der Stock(*-*), storey, floor
der Stoff(*-e*), material, substance, subject-matter
   stöhnen, to groan
das Stöhnen, groaning
   stören, disturb
   stoßen (*stieß, gestoßen*), push, knock, thrust
die Strafanstalt(*-en*), prison
   stramm, strict, rigid, robust
   streng, strict(ly)

   strohblond, flaxen, straw-blond
die Stukkatur, stucco work
   stürzen auf+acc. (*sein*), or *sich — auf*+acc., rush at, plunge at
   stutzen, stop short, hesitate, be startled; trim
   südlich, southern
die Suppe(*-n*), soup
die Suppenschüssel(*-n*), soup dish, tureen

   tadellos, flawless, excellent
die Tagung(*-en*), convention, meeting
die Tasse(*-n*), cup
die Tat(*-en*), deed
der Tatbestand, facts of the case; *den — auf-nehmen* (*-nahm, -genommen*), take down the facts of the case
der Täter(*-*), perpetrator, culprit
   tauchen (*sein, intrans.*), immerse, soak, dive
die Technik, technology, technological achievement
der Techniker(*-*), technician, engineer
der Tee(*-s*), tea
der Teil(*-e*), part
   telefonisch, by telephone
die Terrasse(*-n*), terrace
   teuer, dear
der Teufel(*-*), devil
   theologisch, theological
die Theorie(*-n*), theory
die These(*-n*), thesis, doctrine
das Tischbein(*-e*), table-leg
das Tischchen(*-*), little table
das Tischtuch(*⸚er*), tablecloth
   toben, storm, rage
   tobsüchtig, raving mad

133

das Töchterpensionat(-e), girls' boarding-school
der Tod(-esfälle), death
das Todesurteil(-e), death-sentence
tödlich, deadly, fatal
toll, stupid, senseless; enormous, colossal
die Tortur(-en), torture
der Tote (adj. noun), dead man
töten, kill
die Totenstille, dead silence
tragisch, tragic
die Tragödie(-n), tragedy
die Träne(-n), tear
das Transportgeschäft(-e), transport business
traurig, sad
treffen (traf, getroffen), hit, meet; *Maßnahmen treffen*, to take measures
treiben (trieb, getrieben), drive, push; engage in, carry on
treu, faithful(ly)
trösten, comfort
tröstlich, soothing, comforting
trotz (+gen.), in spite of
trotzdem, nevertheless, in spite of that
trotzig, defiantly
das Tuch(⸚er), cloth
tüchtig, fit, able, capable
die Tür(e)(-n), door

übel, bad, evil
üben, practise
die Überbeschäftigung, overemployment
überflüssig, superfluous
überflüssigerweise, unnecessarily

überfüllen, overfill, overload
über-gehen (-ging, -gegangen; sein), go over to, change to
übergehen (überging, übergangen; haben), pass over, omit
übergeschnappt, turned crazy, 'round the bend'.
überhaupt, in general, by and large, at all
überlassen (überließ, überlassen) (einem etwas), leave to, hand over to
überlegen, consider, ponder over
überlisten, trick, outwit
übernehmen (übernahm, übernommen), take over, take on
übermorgen, the day after tomorrow
überraschen, surprise
übersehen (übersah, übersehen), overlook
über-siedeln, move (residence), transfer
überstreichen (überstrich, überstrichen), paint over
überzeugen, convince
üblich, usual, customary
übrig, remaining, left over; *im übrigen*, for the rest
das Ufer(-), bank, lakeside
ulkig, funny
der Umbau(-ten), building alterations, reconstruction
die Umgebung(-en), surroundings, vicinity
um-gehen (-ging, -gegangen; sein) mit, deal with, handle
um-graben (-grub, -gegraben), dig, turn over (soil)
um-kehren (sein, intrans.), turn round, turn over

um-kippen (*sein*), overturn, capsize
um-kommen (*-kam, -gekommen*; *sein*), perish, die
sich um-schauen, look round (often +*in* + dat.)
umschließen (*umschloß, umschlossen*), enclose, contain
sich um-sehen (*-sah, -gesehen*), look round (often +*in* + dat.)
der *Umstand*(⸚*e*), circumstance; *unter allen Umständen*, in any case, in all circumstances
umstellen, surround
der *Umsturz*(⸚*e*), downfall, overthrow, collapse
um-wandeln, change, transform
die *Umwandlung*(*-en*), change, conversion
unabhängig, independent
unanständig, indecent, improper
unbegreiflich, incomprehensible, inconceivable
unbeholfen, clumsily, awkward(ly), embarrassed
unbeirrbar, imperturbable, unruffled, unerringly
uneigennützig, unselfish(ly)
unendlich, infinite
unermeßlich, immeasurable, immeasurably
unerwartet, unexpected(ly)
der *Unflat*, dirt, filth
unfruchtbar, barren, infertile
ungefährlich, not dangerous, harmless
ungeheuer, enormous(ly), greatly
das *Ungeheuer*(*-*), monster
ungemein, uncommon(ly), unusual(ly)
ungenügend, insufficient, unsatisfactory
ungerufen, uncalled for, gratuitous(ly)
der *Unglaube*(*-ns, -n*), disbelief
das *Unglück* (no pl.), misfortune
der *Unglücksfall*(⸚*e*), accident, mishap
die *Universität*(*-en*), university
der *Unmensch*(*-en, -en*), inhuman creature, monster
unmittelbar, immediate, direct
unmusikalisch, without musical talent
unnötig, unnecessary, unnecessarily
die *Unordnung*, disorder, untidiness
unruhig, restless
unschädlich, harmless
unschuldig, innocent
unsicher, uncertain
unsichtbar, invisible
der *Unsinn*, nonsense, stupidity
unsinnig, absurd
die *Unsumme*(*-n*), enormous sum
unter(+acc. or dat.), under, among
unter-bringen (*-brachte, gebracht*), house, accommodate, shelter
der *Untergang*(⸚*e*), destruction, ruin
unterhalten (*unterhielt, unterhalten*)), entertain; *sich —*, converse, chat
die *Unterkunft*(⸚*e*), accommodation
das *Unternehmen*, undertaking
die *Unternehmung*(*-en*), undertaking, firm

unter-ordnen, subordinate
unterscheiden (*unterschied, unterschieden*), distinguish
das Unterscheidungsvermögen, ability to discriminate
untersuchen, examine, investigate
die Untersuchung(-en), research, investigation
unverändert, unchanged
unverantwortlich, irresponsible
unvoreingenommen, unbiased, without prejudice
unvorstellbar, unimaginable
unwichtig, unimportant
unwürdig (+gen.), unworthy
unzugänglich, inaccessible
das Urteil(-e), judgement, verdict
urteilen, judge

verachten, despise
verändern, alter, change
die Veränderung(-en), alteration, transformation
die Verantwortung(-en), responsibility
der Verband(⸚e), association
verbauen, build up, spoil with buildings
sich verbeugen, bow, make a bow
verbieten (*verbot, verboten*), (*einem etwas*), forbid
verblüfft, amazed, nonplussed
verbotenerweise, against the rules, though it is forbidden
das Verbrechen, crime
der Verbrecher(-), criminal
verbrennen (*verbrannte, verbrannt*), burn
verbringen (*verbrachte, verbracht*), spend (time)

der Verdacht, suspicion; — *schöpfen*, become suspicious
verdanken (*einem etwas*), owe to
verdienen, earn, deserve
verdoppeln, double
sich verdüstern, grow dark, grow gloomy
verehren, respect, admire
der Verfasser(-), author
verfaulen, rot
verfluchen, curse
die Verfügung(-en), disposal; *ich stehe Ihnen zur* —, I am at your disposal
die Vergangenheit, past
vergeblich, vainly, in vain
vergehen (*verging, vergangen; sein*), pass, elapse
das Vergnügen, pleasure, joy
verhaften, arrest
verheeren, ravage, devastate
verhindern, prevent, hinder
die Verirrung(-en), going astray, aberration, delusion
verkannt, misunderstood, not recognized
verklärt, glorified, transfigured
verkochen, boil away, boil to nothing
verkrusten, become encrusted, coated
verlangen, demand
verlassen (*verließ, verlassen*), leave; *sich* — *auf* (+acc.), rely on
der Verlauf(⸚e), course; lapse (time)
verlaufen (*verlief, verlaufen; sein*), take a (its) course, proceed, go
verlegen, embarrassed

verlernen, forget about, unlearn
verleugnen, deny
verloren (p.p. of *verlieren*), lost
verlottert, dilapidated, worse for wear, degenerate
vermeiden (*vermied, vermieden*), avoid
vermögen (*vermochte, vermocht*) *zu* (+inf.), be able to
vermuten, suppose, imagine
die *Vermutung*(*-en*), assumption
vernehmen (*vernahm, vernommen*), examine, interrogate
sich *verneigen*, bend forward, bow
vernichten, destroy, annihilate, abash
die *Vernunft*, reason
vernünftig, reasonable, rational
veröffentlichen, publish
verpesten, pollute, infect, taint
verpflichten, pledge to, bind to
die *Verpflichtung*(*-en*), obligation
der *Verrat*, betrayal, treason
verraten (*verriet, verraten*), betray
verrecken, die, kick the bucket
verrückt, mad
der *Verrückte* (adj. noun), lunatic
die *Verrücktheit*, madness
versagen, fail; cease functioning; deny, refuse
versaufen (*versoff, versoffen; sein*), drown (intrans.) (coll.)
verschieden, various, different
verschließen (*verschloß, verschlossen*), close, lock up
verschlimmern, make worse; sich —, get worse
verschlingen (*verschlang, verschlungen*), swallow up, devour
verschollen, missing, lost without trace
verschweigen (*verschwieg, verschwiegen*), keep secret, keep silent about
verschwinden (*verschwand, verschwunden; sein*), disappear
versetzen, transfer, post, move; pawn
versichern, assure
die *Versicherungsgesellschaft* (*-en*), insurance company
versinken (*versank, versunken; sein*), sink, become engulfed
versorgen, look after, put away, take care of
versprechen (*versprach, versprochen*), promise
der *Verstand*(*=e*), intellect, sense, understanding
verstecken, hide
verstehen (*verstand, verstanden*), understand
sich *verstellen*, pretend
verstorben, deceased, late
verstummen, grow silent, cease talking
der *Versuch*(*-e*), try
versuchen, try
versunken, absorbed, preoccupied
verteilen, distribute, give out
das *Vertrauen*, trust, confidence
vertrottelt, degenerate, feebleminded
der *Verwaltungsrat*(*=e*), board of directors
verwandeln, change
der *Verwandte* (adj. noun), relation

verwechseln, mistake for, mix up
verwirren, confuse, unbalance, disorder
verwundert, astonished, surprised
verzichten auf (+acc.), relinquish, give up claim to, do without
verziert, adorned, decorated
verzweifelt, desperate
die *Verzweiflung*, desperation
der *Vetter*(−n), cousin
vielleicht, perhaps
die *Viertelstunde*(−n), quarter of an hour
die *Villa* (Villen), villa
völlig, completely
vollkommen, completely
voll-kotzen, puke over, be sick all over
vor (+dat.), ago; — *sich hin* (after *starren*, *paffen*, etc.), preoccupied, absorbed, abstractedly
voran-gehen (-ging, -gegangen; sein), precede
voraussehbar, predictable
voraus-sehen (-sah, -gesehen), predict
vor-dringen (-drang, -gedrungen; sein), penetrate into, forward
der *Vorfall*(⸚e), occurrence, event
vor-fallen (-fiel, -gefallen; sein) happen, take place
vor-geben (-gab, -gegeben), pretend
das *Vorgefallene* (adj. noun), previous happenings
vor-gehen (-ging, -gegangen; sein), go forward, proceed

vorhanden, at hand, present
der *Vorhang*(⸚e), curtain
die *Vorhangkordel*(−n), curtain pull-rope
vorher, before, previously
sich *vor-kämpfen*, fight one's way forward
vor-kommen (-kam, -gekommen; sein), occur, happen
vorne, at the front
sich *vor-nehmen* (-nahm, -genommen), resolve, intend, undertake
der *Vorschein*, appearance
vor-spielen, play (to an audience)
vor-stellen, introduce; *sich —*, imagine; introduce oneself
vorüber, past
der *Vorwurf*(⸚e), reproach, blame
vor-ziehen (-zog, -gezogen), prefer
vorzüglich, excellent

die *Waffe*(−n), weapon
der *Wagen*(−), trolley, cart, car
wählen, choose
wahnsinnig, mad, insane
wahr, true
während, while; (+gen.), during
die *Wahrheit*(−en), truth
wahr-nehmen (-nahm, -genommen), observe, perceive, take (opportunity)
der *Waisenbub*(−en, −en), orphan child
walten, govern, hold sway, prevail
die *Wand*(⸚e), wall
warten auf (+acc.), wait for
der *Wärter*(−), keeper, guard
warum, why

VOCABULARY

weder ... noch, neither ... nor
das Weib(-er), woman
weiden, graze
sich weigern (zu + inf.), refuse
weise, wise
die Weise(-n), way, manner, tune
weisen (wies, gewiesen) auf (+acc.), point to
die Weisheit(-en), wisdom
der Weißwein(-e), white wine
weit, wide, broad, far
weitaus, by far, much
weiter, further
weiter-blühen, continue to bloom
weiterhin, furthermore
weitläufig, extensive
das Weltall, cosmos
weltbekannt, well-known, famous
die Weltherrschaft, world dominion
der Weltraum, outer space
der Weltraumfahrer(-), space-traveller
der Weltruf, international repute, world fame
das Weltunternehmen, world undertaking
wenden (wandte, gewandt, or weak), to turn
die Wendung(-en), turning, turn
wenn auch, even though
werfen (warf, geworfen), throw
die Werkpolizei, works police
wert, worth, valued; *nicht der Rede —,* not worth speaking of
das Wesen, being, existence, essence
weshalb, why? for what reason?

wichtig, serious, important
widmen, dedicate
wieso?, how? but why? why is it?
willen: um einer Sache willen, for the sake of something
Willkommen heißen (hieß, geheißen), welcome
winken, beckon, wave
wirklich, real(ly)
die Wirklichkeit, reality
wirksam, effective(ly)
die Wirtschaft(-en), inn; economy
der Wirtschaftsführer(-), business magnate, tycoon
das Wissen, knowledge
die Wissenschaft(-en), knowledge, science
der Wissenschaftler(-), scientist
wissenschaftlich, scientific, in a scientific manner
der Witwer(-), widower
der Witz(-e), joke, wit
das Wohl, health, welfare
womöglich, wherever possible, if possible
das Wunder(-), miracle
der Wunsch(⸚e), wish
wünschen, wish
würdig (+gen.), worthy
die Wüste(-n), desert
wütend, furious, angry

zahlen, pay
zählen, count
die Zahntechnikerschule(-n), dental school, school for dental mechanics
zaubern, charm, produce magical effects
zeigen, show

die Zeit(*-en*), **time**
das Zeitalter, **age,** period
der Zentralheizungskörper(-), radiator
zerschlissen, **worn,** threadbare
zerstören, destroy
ziehen (*zog, gezogen*), draw, pull (*haben*); go, proceed (*sein*)
das Ziel(*-e*), goal, aim
ziemlich, fairly, somewhat
die Zigarrenkiste(*-n*), cigar-box
das Zivil, plain clothes
das Zuchthaus(*⸚er*), prison
zuerst, first of all, firstly
der Zufall(*⸚e*), chance
zufällig, by chance
zufälligerweise, by chance
zu-flüstern (+ dat.), whisper to
zufrieden mit, satisfied with
zu-geben (*-gab, -gegeben*), admit, confess
der Zug(*⸚e*), train; trait, feature
der Zuhälter(-), pimp, procurer
die Zukunft, future
zu-lassen (*-ließ, gelassen*), allow, admit
zu-nicken (+ dat.), nod to
zurück-denken, (*-dachte, -gedacht*), think back
zurück-führen auf (+ acc.): *das ist auf ... zurückzuführen,* is owing to, is caused by

zurück-kehren (*sein*), return
zurück-stecken, stick back, put back
sich zurück-ziehen (*-zog, -gezogen*), withdraw
das Zusammenbrechen, collapse
zusammen-gehören, belong together
der Zusammenhang(*⸚e*), connection
zusätzlich, additional
der Zuschauer(-), spectator
zu-schaufeln, shovel over to, hand over to
der Zustand(*⸚e*), condition
zuteil: *einem — werden,* fall to a person's lot
zuvor-kommen (*-kam, -gekommen; sein*) (+ dat.), anticipate, do first
zu-wenden (*wandte, gewandt,* or weak), turn to
zu-winken (+ dat.), beckon to, wave to
der Zwang, restraint, force; *sich — an-tun,* restrain oneself
zwar, indeed, to be sure.
der Zweck(*-e*), aim, end, purpose; *zu welchem —?* for what purpose?
der Zweifel(-), doubt
zweifeln an (+ dat.), be doubtful of
zwingen (*zwang, gezwungen*), compel